PEOPLE, PLANTS, AND PATENTS

Funding Organizations for the Crucible Project

Australian Centre for International Agricultural Research
(ACIAR, Australia)

Directorate General for International Cooperation
(DGIS, Netherlands)

International Development Research Centre
(IDRC, Canada)

Swedish Agency for Research Cooperation with
Developing Countries
(SAREC, Sweden)

Swiss Development Corporation
(SDC, Switzerland)

Partner Organizations

International Plant Genetics Resources Institute
(IPGRI, Italy)

Rural Advancement Foundation International
(RAFI, Canada)

PEOPLE, PLANTS, AND PATENTS

THE IMPACT OF INTELLECTUAL PROPERTY ON BIODIVERSITY, CONSERVATION, TRADE, AND RURAL SOCIETY

The Crucible Group

INTERNATIONAL DEVELOPMENT RESEARCH CENTRE

Ottawa • Cairo • Dakar • Johannesburg • Montevideo • Nairobi • New Delhi • Singapore

Published by the International Development Research Centre
PO Box 8500, Ottawa, ON, Canada K1G 3H9

Crucible Group

People, plants, and patents : the impact of intellectual property on biodiversity, conservation, trade, and rural society. Ottawa, ON, IDRC, 1994. xxii + 118 p. : ill.

/Intellectual property/, /legal protection/, /biotechnology/, /plant resources/, /genetic resources/, /resources conservation/ — /policy making/, /decision making/, /social participation/, /patents/, /conventions/, /trade agreements/, /recommendations/, references.

UDC: 347.77:574   ISBN: 0-88936-725-6

A microfiche edition is available.

Printed in Canada

Contents

PREFACE

THE CRUCIBLE GROUP

The Crucible Group members represent the widest cross section of sociopolitical perspectives and agricultural experience that may have ever been assembled to hammer out ideas and recommendations on this hotly contentious subject. Among those who sat together at the first meeting from 16 to 21 June in Uppsala, Sweden, and from 28 September to 1 October 1993 in Bern, Switzerland, were those who oppose all forms of intellectual property protection over life forms. Equally present were those who are exponents of the social benefits of intellectual property. Between these two traditional "opposites" were still others with a wide mix of views and experiences. The Crucible Group includes grassroots organizers working with small-scale or subsistence farmers, agricultural research scientists and science managers, intellectual property specialists, trade diplomats, and agricultural policy analysts from South and North and from government and industry.

From the beginning, the Crucible Group recognized that its membership embodied fundamental differences of opinion and acknowledged the thought and sincerity behind all of these opinions and the integrity of those holding them. Nevertheless, the Group members shared a number of concerns and convictions that made it important for them to work together.

This report was never intended to become a consensus document. The Crucible Group agreed that they would struggle together to identify trends, concerns, and opportunities on intellectual property issues relevant to plant breeding and plant genetic resources. After extended discussions and intense exchanges, the Group has been surprised to discover many areas of shared opinion and a common sense of urgency. This report is still not a consensus document — far from it. It is, as it was intended, an effort to assist policymakers and opinion makers in an extraordinarily important, fast-changing, and politicized field to identify the major points and the range of policy alternatives that can reasonably be pursued.

The Crucible Group itself has not completed its task. Together with the sponsoring organizations, the Group is committed to continue monitoring trends in intellectual property and to make themselves available to organizations and governments to advise on policy issues. The intellectual property debate will be with us for many years to come and the Crucible Project intends to be a constructive contributor to that debate.

The members of the Crucible Group come from public and private research institutions, nongovernmental organizations (NGOs), governments, and academia. It was agreed that because each member is participating in his or her individual capacity, organization or company affiliations would not be included. The Crucible Group is:

FORMAL SECTOR RESEARCH INSTITUTIONS

Bo Bengtsson, Sweden
Tewolde Berhan G. Egziabher, Ethiopia
Jaap Hardon, Netherlands
Bente Herstad, Norway
Klaus Lampe, Germany
Vo-Tong Xuan, Vietnam

INFORMAL SECTOR RESEARCH INSTITUTIONS

Henk Hobbelink, Spain
Camila Montecinos, Chile
Andrew Mushita, Zimbabwe
Bob Phelps, Australia
Michel Pimbert, Switzerland
Sarojeni Rengam, Malaysia
Rene Salazar, Philippines

COMMERCIAL AND ACADEMIC

Carlos Correa, Argentina
Don Duvick, USA
Katy Moran, USA
Tim Roberts, UK

TRADE AND POLICY

Erskine Childers, Ireland
Sven Hamrell, Sweden
Amir Jamal, Tanzania
Francisco Martinez-Gomez, Mexico

CRUCIBLE PROJECT MANAGEMENT COMMITTEE

Geoff Hawtin, IPGRI (Chair)
Pat Roy Mooney, RAFI (Coordinator)
Paul Egger, SDC, Switzerland
Chusa Gines, IDRC, Canada
George Rothschild, ACIAR, Australia
Carl-Gustaf Thornstrom, SAREC, Sweden
Hans Wessels, DGIS, Netherlands

ACKNOWLEDGMENTS

During the years 1988 to 1991, a series of informal meetings took place under the title of the Keystone International Dialogue on Plant Genetic Resources. Its final plenary report (Keystone Center 1991) recommended sweeping changes and increased support for the conservation of plant genetic resources. Although widely applauded, the Keystone initiative fell short in addressing the critical policy concerns related to intellectual property over biomaterials. Thus, when a number of Keystone "veterans" met in Nairobi late in 1992, talk turned to their unfinished business and the notion of a "Crucible" Group to debate the intellectual property (IP) agenda.

In arcane English, a crucible is a boiling pot used to distill diverse elements. Those gathered in Nairobi (Jaap Hardon, Geoff Hawtin, Henk Hobbelink, Pat Mooney, and Andrew Mushita) thought the title appropriate for an informal group of diverse individuals who could be charged with the task of distilling viewpoints and recommendations on this issue under pressure of an urgent deadline. The proposal was to produce a nonconsensus document helpful to policy and opinion-makers within 12 months. The first informal meeting of the Group took place at the end of April 1993. One year later, and with the help of many, this "work in progress" has resulted. It does not entirely satisfy any member of the Crucible Group or of the Management Committee, but we all acknowledge that it represents an important contribution to the international debate and one which should be shared at this time.

Financial and programmatic support for the Project has come from many sources. The International Development Research Centre (IDRC) of Canada generously agreed to provide both financial support and the invaluable advice of Chusa Gines as a member of the Management Committee. The Swedish Agency for Research Cooperation with Developing Countries (SAREC), provided the advice of Carl-Gustaf Thornstrom and also arranged with Sven Hamrell, then Director of the Dag Hammarskjold Foundation, for the first full meeting of the Crucible Group in Uppsala. Likewise, Paul Egger and Jurg Benz of the Swiss Development Corporation (SDC) joined the Management Committee and hosted the second full meeting in Bern. George Rothschild of the Australian Centre for International Agricultural Research (ACIAR) also provided financial support as a member of the Management Committee.

The Crucible Project does not end with this report. Given the changing global IP situation, in the wake of the recent GATT agreements and the entry into force of the Convention on Biological Diversity, the Group intends to continue to monitor trends and advise on IP as a service to countries and institutions that request support. The Directorate General for International Cooperation (DGIS) of the Netherlands is providing substantial additional support to allow this initial work to continue and Hans Wessels of DGIS has joined the Management Committee for this purpose.

The Management Committee wishes to thank all those mentioned above and the many individuals who contributed to this Project. To Beverly Cross of the Rural Advancement Foundation International (RAFI) and Sheilah Ebel of the International Plant Genetics Resources Institute (IPGRI) for their invaluable liaison and administrative roles. To Don Duvick, Tewolde Berhan G. Egziabher, Henk Hobbelink, Camila Montecinos, and Tim Roberts, who did so much of the drafting, and to Kathy Kealey, who took on the task of the final technical edit.

The Project has indeed turned out to have justified the name "Crucible," and we hope the distilled essence will prove of value to those involved in the complex and politically charged process of developing appropriate systems for promoting innovation and protecting intellectual property as it relates to plant genetic resources.

EXECUTIVE SUMMARY

In the closing decade of the 20th century, changed political forces and the advent of new technologies, especially biotechnologies and informatics, have contributed to the development of a global marketplace. New technologies are an important consideration in both national development and international trade. This influence has driven a revolution in intellectual property (IP) systems. Innovation and research are a strong new presence in world affairs. Every country, South and North, will be affected by the new and integrated role played by IP in all aspects of development and the environment. For the South, in particular, the impact of IP on farmers, rural societies, and on biological (including genetic) diversity will be profoundly important.

Perhaps for the first time, policymakers and opinon makers dealing with trade, development planning, agriculture, and the environment must give careful consideration to the implications of intellectual property. Many will be surprised to find that IP decisions have major implications for national food security, agricultural and rural development, and for environmental conservation.

The purpose of this report is to identify key issues and choices and to describe the broader context within which decisions are being made. The full report contains 28 consensus recommendations that are clearly marked in appropriately titled boxes at the end of the sections to which they relate. (The recommendations are also summarized in this section in similar boxes.) In addition, the Group is including a number of other boxes titled "Different Viewpoints." In each case, three different opinions are expressed that represent the range of opinions expressed within the Group on the subject. Although we may not agree with one another, we do concur that each of the different opinions expressed could be considered by policymakers en route to decisions. We hope you find this unique summary of the major debating points helpful.

THE POLICY ENVIRONMENT

A number of factors are coming together to make intellectual property and biodiversity important issues for humanity. First, one of the most persistent and growing political realities of the past quarter-century is public awareness of environmental degradation. Although the "popularity" of environmental issues can be seen to wax and wane somewhat before and after major events, such as the Earth Summit of 1992 (the United Nations Conference on Environment and Development, UNCED), there is an intensifying awareness in global civil society that all is not well and that strong actions must be taken. We believe there is indeed cause for alarm and nowhere more so than for the food crops and medicinal plants that nurture us.

With the spread of environmental awareness, there is an increased understanding that biodiversity is also the biomaterial we need to overcome new dangers and to meet new opportunities. Greenhouse gases, climate change, and ozone depletion portend unpredictable shifts in disease patterns for people, livestock, and crops. Access to abundant genetic diversity will be the key to human survival. If diversity goes, we will soon follow.

Simultaneously, human genius and innovation are bringing about a remarkable revolution in the use of biomaterials. New biotechnologies can use biodiversity in ways it has never been used before. Although there are mixed opinions as to the ethics and safety of genetic manipulation, and how quickly products are coming to market, there is general recognition among policymakers and opinion makers that this is a new social and economic force to be reckoned with.

On the one hand, the world has a declining resource base of biomaterials and, on the other hand, a rising demand for, and competence with, biological (especially genetic) resources. This could seem to be a recipe for economic benefit and a clear case for conservation. The benefits of genetic conservation, however, are long term and rarely predictable. Commercial profit horizons are short term and depend on predictability. We cannot expect conservation to yield windfall rewards in the immediate future.

It is certain that no country has cornered the market on biodiversity. No country is even remotely self-sufficient in its needs for genetic resources. Genetic diversity is full of surprises. Some of the most biologically diverse regions in the world may depend upon much less diverse regions for some of their most important foods and medicines. The world needs a strong multilateral framework within which nation-states can manage their resources and negotiate their access.

These broad factors are brought into focus by the adoption of the new GATT accord and the coming-into-force of the Convention on Biological Diversity. Intellectual property is now firmly entrenched in the trade agreement, and continues to be a controversial topic on the biodiversity agenda. In this context of change and uncertainty, recent developments make it clear that IP is not a static mechanism for invention but a changing market mechanism that can significantly influence public- and private-sector relationships. It can also profoundly influence the well-being of rural societies. Governments, rural and indigenous communities, and industry must determine how to address the issue of IP. Intellectual property policies could set the framework for how we approach the conservation and development of biodiversity. In the absence of a convincing global morality, strong national policies are imperative. The general environment of concern and uncertainty lead to the Report's first major recommendation.

Sensing, on the one hand, a certain uncertainty and lack of understanding related to intellectual property regimes and, on the other hand, the opportunity to create a new covenant in support of wider innovative processes, the Crucible Group recommends that the United Nations convene an international conference on society and innovation. Now, and at this conference, policymakers must bear in mind that some people, countries, and cultures have deep ethical concerns about biotechnology and the concept of life patenting.

NURTURING DIVERSITY

The process that has brought about the Convention on Biological Diversity has served to highlight that rural and indigenous communities have both technical competence and knowledge needed to conserve plant genetic resources. Conservation strategies that begin with local communities have perhaps the best chance to work. The logical beginning point in the development of a practical, national conservation and enhancement program is the participation of communities in partnership with institutions in the formal sector.

It must be understood, however, that, for farmers, extinction can take place when seed leaves the field. That it is stored in a genebank is not necessarily a guarantee that farmers will ever see it, or its progeny, again. Conservation programs and genebanks must establish a new relationship with rural communities that guarantees farmers access to the germplasm they are prepared to share. At the same time, a conservation strategy must engage the private sector as well as public-sector institutions. Industry can make a constructive contribution. This gives rise to our second general recommendation.

> The Crucible Group stresses the primacy of specific national conservation strategies for plant genetic resources that invite the participation of local communities as well as private companies. Holders of *ex situ* germplasm collections should develop equitable partnerships with indigenous and rural societies and make their collections available to them.

There is great hope that the Biodiversity Convention will become the cornerstone of a multilateral commitment to the equitable conservation and enhancement of biological diversity. There are two outstanding sets of issues that relate very closely. The first is the status of *ex situ* collections of biomaterials gathered before the Convention. Perhaps two-thirds of all crop germplasm now in storage is not in the country from which it was collected. Some Group members believe that if the Convention only safeguards that which we do not know to exist and do not know to have value, it will have failed to achieve one of its primary goals of linking biodiversity with development.

The second set of issues relate to Farmers' Rights (that is, a recognition of the rights of farmers to compensation for their contribution to plant genetic resources) and industry's concern that IP for biomaterials be protected. Some see the Convention as a kind of "fast GATT" for IP proponents. Others view the Convention as a sidetrack for IP opponents to pirate private research; hence, our third general recommendation.

> The uncertainty regarding the status of *ex situ* biomaterial collections must be addressed in these early days of the Convention. Similarly, the Crucible Group recommends that the outstanding issues of Farmers' Rights and of IP be clarified. The Biodiversity Convention may find that the Fourth International Technical Conference on Plant Genetic Resources (Berlin, June 1996) offers the best negotiating process and forum for the resolution of these issues.

Diversifying Innovation

If the issue facing decision-makers is how to respond to a new trading environment that involves IP rules, the opportunity at hand is to rethink the place of innovation in a national and global context. In this era of the "information highway," the real challenge is to make it a two-way street that ensures the safety of passengers going each way. On one side, we have indigenous and other rural communities (the informal system of innovation) and, on the other side, we have public and private institutes of research (formal innovators). One side has a profound "macrobiological" understanding of their microenvironment. The other has a strong "microbiological" understanding of their macroenvironment. The task is to allow the two to cooperate without violating their rights or capacities. Farmers' fields and forests are laboratories. Farmers and healers are researchers. Every season is an experiment. Scientists should be partners. If we are going to conserve and develop diversity, these two systems need each other.

To become full partners in the innovation process, community innovation requires Germplasm, Information, Funds, Technologies, and Systems. These are the "GIFTS" that turn plant genetic diversity into a resource and a gift from generations of farming societies to generations yet unborn. This implies an obligation to farmers and some important prerequisites for an innovation policy.

> The Crucible Group agrees that innovation strategies should promote decentralization, diversity, and democracy at all levels, rather than only promoting centralization, uniformity, and control. Current IP systems are ineffective in supporting community-level innovation.

If the community role is the new discovery in innovation, partnership must be the new motto. We must create the new covenant that allows all researchers to associate in transparent and equitable ways that support intellectual integrity. This includes the private sector. Any national program that does not seek to exploit the creative role of the private sector fails to capitalize on a vital opportunity.

> The Crucible Group recommends the development of national innovation strategies for the use of biomaterials that are tailored to national needs and opportunities. The outstanding challenge is to create equitable policies and initiatives that facilitate collaboration between formal (public and private institutions) and informal (community) sectors. The creative contribution of private initiatives (cooperative or company) should not be neglected.

DIVINING THE TRADE OPTIONS

With respect to IP, the GATT agreement obliges signatory states to adopt either a patent or some form of *sui generis* (that is, of its own kind, constituting a class alone, unique, peculiar) IP system for plant varieties. Policymakers have a number of choices depending on their view of IP. Governments can adopt patent laws for plant varieties or they can take on either one of two forms of Plant Breeders' Rights (PBR) (the 1978 or the 1991 Conventions) under the Union for the Protection of New Varieties of Plants (UPOV). Alternatively, they can devise some other form of *sui generis* legislation, such as the United Nations Educational, Scientific and Cultural Organisation–World Intellectual Property Organization (Unesco–WIPO) Model Provisions on Folklore or Inventors' Certificates. Another option, in a fast-changing world, is to take advantage of the coming 4 or 5 years to monitor IP developments and make a policy decision sometime before the GATT provisions come under review.

It is important to realize that the GATT accord is a flexible document open to many kinds of interpretation. Much of the language is general in nature and there is an ambiguous provision for exemption for environmental reasons.

Among the many points of debate is whether or not the patent system is self-correcting or whether a larger segment of society needs to become a participant in the unfolding process. There are strong opinions on both sides of this debate. Other observers suggest that biotechnology may warrant its own *sui generis* IP system, such as those developed for computer software and integrated circuit technologies.

> Under the pressure of possible exclusion from an encompassing global trade agreement, many countries feel pressed to adopt some form of IP protection for plant varieties. The Crucible Group concurs that compulsion is inappropriate and that countries, obviously, have every right to protect their environment and the well-being of their peoples if they feel that trade rules threaten their security.

Patents provide a very strong protection for inventors. Many observers believe that the patent system has the flexibility to adapt to changing circumstances, and that it will be the preferred system of protection for those developing new biotechnologies. Others believe that a system intended to protect light bulbs and sewing machines cannot readily be applied to living materials. Genes in plant varieties are particularly difficult to control, and some regard protection for genetic material to be extremely difficult to realize. Contrary to the understanding of some policymakers, GATT does not require patents for plant varieties. There is general agreement that the development of conventional plant varieties does not require patent protection.

> The Crucible Group notes that it is not necessary to establish patent legislation for plant varieties to meet GATT requirements or the needs of plant breeders. It recommends that those pursuing a patent model ensure that the research exemption is strong and clear. It also advises that gene flows between plant populations are often uncontrollable and that patent regulation could prove difficult.

The Union for the Protection of New Varieties of Plants is a form of *sui generis* protection for plant varieties often known as Plant Breeders' Rights or Plant Variety Protection (PBR, PVP). Until 31 December 1995, any country may choose to join either the UPOV

Convention of 1978 or the UPOV Convention of 1991. After 1995, the 1978 Convention will no longer accept new members, although states adhering to this version may remain and will still be recognized as member states of UPOV in good standing. The 1978 UPOV Convention allows governments to determine the species they wish to protect and ensures that farmers can save and exchange seed for the next growing season. The 1991 Convention requires that all plant species must be protected and does not permit farmers to save or exchange protected seed. Both models have advantages and drawbacks, depending on the country and the point of view. Presumably, governments could adopt legislation compatible with UPOV 1978 after 1995 and, although not joining UPOV, could still be in good standing with the international community and in keeping with the GATT agreement.

In general, the South is not a target for GATT's IP provisions for plant varieties. With exceptions, countries have both time and choices. Private companies are not interested in obliging small-scale farmers not to save company-protected seed for succeeding generations or even in preventing them from trading seed with their neighbours. Breeders will not prosper unless farmers do. Many companies believe that strong breeders' rights could increase genetic diversity and farmer security.

Another means of meeting GATT requirements is with the adoption of PBRs through either the 1978 or 1991 UPOV Conventions. The Crucible Group agrees that UPOV 1978 gives countries greater flexibility. Countries are advised that related seeds legislation, such as National Lists (regulating the quality of seed and range of varieties available to farmers), could have adverse effects in the presence of PVP.

There has been a distressing lack of innovative thinking about Innovation Systems. In leaving the door open to *sui generis* forms of IP for plant varieties, GATT invites industry, farmers, and governments to respond creatively.

This creativity is urgently needed. Intellectual Property systems have evolved within a certain legal and cultural context that renders their protection inaccessible to most informal innovators most of the time. There are also obvious economic and logistical barriers to the protection of indigenous knowledge. Intellectual Property Systems that do not make space for informal innovators are fundamentally inequitable. This shortcoming can lead to abuse and must be addressed.

Among the possibilities that could be considered are modifications to existing IP Systems that make way for community protection, including the development of public defenders within patent offices, gene-tracking databases, and review mechanisms that could bring some support to the informal sector. The WIPO–Unesco Folklore Provisions, first drafted in 1985, could possibly give communities rights over their evolutionary biological inventions for as long as they continue to innovate. This and other options could be pursued.

Because the various systems of IP are evolving, proponents and opponents should not make the mistake of denying the possibility of beneficial changes. Some opponents of IP, for example, might prefer a system without exclusive monopoly provisions. Various forms of licencing are also possible. There may be instruments available that would encourage innovation and, nevertheless, strengthen society's right and ability to use innovation.

> The Crucible Group acknowledges that GATT requirements and the national need for an innovation strategy, or both, may be served through some form of *sui generis* legislation that may or may not involve IP. Given that states have several years to develop legislation under the GATT rules, the various options deserve closer study.

The CGIAR's International Centres find themselves in a unique position. The Centres hold an estimated 40% of the unique food-crop germplasm in *ex situ* storage in the world. These same Centres are the world's major distributors of enhanced germplasm for national (public and private) breeding programs in the South.

The Centres also breed their own varieties, which they make available free to farmers in the South.

The Centres are caught in a dilemma. They believe that the germplasm they hold is theirs "in trust" on behalf of the world and, particularly, on behalf of developing countries. They wish to exchange breeding material as fully and freely as possible. Their material — about a half million germplasm accessions — was almost all collected before the coming into force of the Convention on Biodiversity. In a sense, the International Centres are "a-lateral" institutes caught between two "multilateral" accords (GATT and the Convention) that press governments to develop "bilateral" relationships for both the conservation and the use of plant genetic resources.

It is clear that the Centres must have open and well-defined policies to ensure that any benefit from direct exploitation of germplasm held by then in trust accrues to the countries that donate the germplasm. It is also important that Centres negotiate access to new technologies being developed in the North that could be of use in the South.

With respect to the status of *ex situ* collections, the Crucible Group welcomes the joint initiative of the Food and Agriculture Organization of the United Nations (FAO) and member institutes of the Consultative Group on International Agricultural Research (CGIAR) to establish an "in-trust" agreement for the benefit of developing countries. The Group further recommends that CGIAR's international centres establish a transparent IP policy that uses Material Transfer Agreements (MTAs) so that the benefits arising from the direct use of in-trust genetic materials accrue to the countries that donate the material. Holders of germplasm collections should also give serious consideration to the use of MTAs and to Defensive Publication provisions in some patent legislation that could help to ensure the secure availability of collections. The Group is concerned, however, that a trend toward bilateral germplasm agreements could undercut beneficial multilateral accords. There is a need to ensure strong multilateral mechanisms as umbrellas to bilateral arrangements.

1. POLICY

THE CHANGING INTERNATIONAL FRAMEWORK

The Rio Earth Summit of 1992 may become known as one the most important international conferences of this century. Future generations will acknowledge two critical accomplishments: through Agenda 21, humanity has given itself not a blueprint but a timetable for survival; and a hopeful process of discovery, debate, and participation has begun. If on-the-ground work results, then those who trod the long road to Rio de Janeiro will deserve great praise.

In the multitude of vital issues highlighted during the Rio Summit, none drew more attention than the global need to conserve biological diversity. Few environmental concerns are more universally acknowledged. Scientific and social opinion are united in understanding that humanity is in the process of squandering an incalculably important resource central to our food, health, and economic security.

Faced with such common concern, most delegates to the Rio conference, as well as the world community, were surprised by the intense debate that arose around the Convention on Biological Diversity and its connection to IP. Although some governments left Rio convinced that IP (usually understood to be patents) is the main tool of a new technological colonialism, other delegations left viewing patents as a powerful instrument of national economic liberation. Probably most negotiators could be forgiven for assuming that IP is a single, probably inflexible, system that must either be adopted or rejected.

There is also diversity within IP, however; it has its kingdoms and genera. As we find in nature, IP is capable of evolution and mutation. Although, as the authors of this report, we share the whole range of views expressed in Rio on the role of IP, and view its changes with either optimism or alarm, we urge all policy- and opinion-makers to examine IP with great care. Those who reviewed patent law a few decades ago may not recognize it today. What IP will become tomorrow will be up to the descendants of Rio.

In preparing this report, we debated among ourselves whether IP would develop into the most important and economically inexpensive instrument available to the South to stimulate innovation and technology transfer. Or, conversely, whether IP would become an unwieldy, resource-draining, and devastating instrument of foreign control. We do agree that any policy on IP related to biodiversity must be determined within the context of national needs and as part of a wider national strategy to promote science, innovation, and conservation. We are aware that nations do not live in the world alone and that national policies must survive within a regional and global political framework not often of their own choosing. In the absence of a reliable global morality, however, we give the greatest importance to national self-determination. National policy, we conclude, must be developed bearing in mind the importance of conservation for development, the changing role of IP in world commerce, and the place of innovation in human progress.

> *In the absence of a convincing Global Morality, strong national policies are imperative.*

THE GROWING IMPORTANCE OF PLANT BIODIVERSITY

The advent of new biotechnologies and the capacity to identify and incorporate exotic genetic material into commercial products has forced the pace of change in industry and in IP systems. Researchers are discovering new ways to use old biomaterials, and the role of biomaterials for food, health, and other industrial purposes is expanding significantly. These new market opportunities have catalyzed additional research and investment. However, critically, the new technologies and the new hope for sustainability depend upon society's access to, and use of, a wide range of genetic materials.

Industrial Biomaterials

In manufacturing, some analysts are projecting that plants could recapture the share of the total industrial materials market they enjoyed in the 1920s and that a full one-third of all such materials could be derived not from petroleum-based stocks but from plant resources (Morris and Ahmed 1992). Handled correctly, the environmental and social benefits could be considerable. Much of the new market could accrue to tropical and subtropical regions.

Medicinal Plants

In the health field, 80% of the world's population is at least partly dependent upon traditional medicine and medicinal plants to treat their ills (Shelton 1993). The conservation of pharmaceutical biodiversity is critical. More than two-thirds of the world's plant species — at least

Greenhouse gases, climate change, and ozone depletion mean unpredictable shifts in disease patterns for people, livestock, and crops. Access to abundant genetic diversity will be the key to human survival. If diversity goes, we will be soon to follow.

35 000 of which have potential medicinal value — originate in developing countries (Quiambao 1992) (Figure 1). According to an intergovernmental meeting of Southern experts in Tanzania in 1990, at least 7 000 medical compounds in the Western pharmacopoeia — from aspirin to birth control pills — are drawn from plants (Mshigenio 1990). The estimated value (manufacturer's price) of the South's medicinal materials could range from $35 billion to $47 billion by the year 2000 (UNEP 1992) (monetary values are in US dollars throughout this book). Because the development of medicinal plants relies heavily on the knowledge of indigenous peoples and rural societies, concerns about equitable benefit sharing and IP inevitably arise.

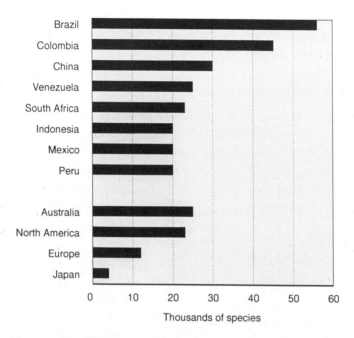

Figure 1. Plant biodiversity: a comparison, by number of species, of
major regions (source: Davis et al. 1986; WRI 1992,
cited in Cunningham 1993).

Agricultural Biodiversity

In the case of agriculture, it is simply impossible to offer a reasonable estimate for the contribution of genetic diversity to crop
production. The agricultural research community cannot guarantee the long-term survival of any crop, in any country, if the
breeding options for that crop are curtailed through the nonavail-
ability of cultivated or so-called wild germplasm. Humanity shares
a common bowl containing only 20 cultivated crops that sustain
90% of our calorie requirements (FAO 1991). All 20 crops originate
in developing countries. All are alarmingly vulnerable to pests and
diseases and depend on genetic diversity for their continued survival. During this century, most authorities believe that an alarming proportion of the genetic variability of our major food plants

— as it is available in the field — has become extinct. The conservation and development of the remaining crop diversity is a matter of vital global concern.

Although there is no doubt that today's conservation of biological diversity will yield considerable economic and social benefit in the years ahead, we recognize that the economic gains will grow slowly, that there will be few financial "windfalls," and that only those countries that have both conservation and development strategies for biodiversity are likely to reap significant rewards.

There will be both domestic and foreign market opportunities arising from the nurturing of biodiversity. The foreign market potential, for the South, is probably greatest with medicinal plants or in the development of specific genetic characteristics for high-value export crops, for example, for beverages, spices, and confectioneries. This could lead some countries to overlook the more immediate application of biomaterials for domestic purposes, forgetting perhaps that the diversity exists locally because it "fits" ecologically and is backed by local knowledge and experience with its uses. Especially in the case of farmers' varieties and medicinal plants, national development may derive the greatest benefit and lead logically to a later expansion to international markets.

> *The benefits of genetic conservation are long term and rarely predictable. Commercial profit horizons are short term and depend on predictability. We cannot expect conservation to yield windfall rewards in the immediate future.*

It is humbling, but important, for us to remember that no country or region can "corner the market" on biodiversity. Neither is any country or region self-sufficient in biomaterials. The last several centuries have witnessed a kind of botanical chess game in which staple foods and high-value export crops have been positioned and repositioned about the globe as markets and opportunities shift. Table 1, for example, shows that even for a country as botanically abundant as Brazil, almost two-thirds of human calorie

Table 1. Sources of plant-derived calories in Brazil.

Crop	Share of plant-derived calories (%)	Centre of origin
Sugar	20.38	Indochina
Rice (paddy)	17.64	Asia
Wheat	15.29	West and Central Asia
Maize	12.20	Central America
Soybean	8.84	China–Japan
Cassava	7.10	Brazil–Paraguay
Beans	6.40	Andes
Bananas	2.22	Indochina

Source: FAO Food Balance Sheets (1984–86).

intake, from plants, is drawn from species whose genetic origins are on another continent.

Even the most biologically independent countries look to other regions of the world for a crucial share of their genetic stocks (Kloppenburg 1988). Wheat, for example, originated in the Near East, but the specific genes that inspired semidwarf wheats and propelled the Green Revolution came from Japan via the United States and Mexico, and disease-resistant genes found recently in Central America may support crop yields as far away as India. Bananas and plantains are most important as cash crops in South and Central America and the highest per capita consumption as a staple food is in East Africa; however, "home" for bananas and plantains is in Southeast Asia.

Our genetic interdependence is even greater when we consider export commodities. Although the world's primary source of natural rubber originated in Brazil, the centre of production and of many new innovations is in Southeast Asia. Biotechnology companies are currently evaluating other latex-bearing plants with origins as scattered as India and Mexico (*Industrial Bioprocessing* 1993). Southeast Asia is also the centre of production for oil palm, although the crop's gene centre lies in tropical Africa. The centre of origin for the Latin American coffee industry is Ethiopia, and East Africa's sisal production is based upon germplasm from Central

America. The famous rosy periwinkle, a plant vital to childhood leukemia treatment, originated in, and has long been used by, healers in Madagascar. It was actually commercialized by Eli Lilly from germplasm gathered in the Philippines and Jamaica (Cunningham 1993).

In view of our interdependence, it is obvious that national conservation and enhancement strategies must be supported by a global plant genetic resources system. Our interdependence also reaches to the relationship between scientific institutions — here

> *Genetic diversity is full of surprises. We need each other. No country is independent.*

described as the "formal" innovation system — and indigenous and rural peoples, who make up the "community" innovation system. Clearly, the national and world communities benefit enormously from the scientific knowledge and conservation expertise of community innovators. Simultaneously, rural societies can benefit from science and innovation in the formal sector and from access to "exotic" biodiversity for local experimentation. Concern arises, however, when equal partners have an unequal opportunity to benefit — or where it appears that IP is available only to formal innovators, sometimes at the expense of community innovators.

THE CHANGING ROLE OF INTELLECTUAL PROPERTY

Intellectual property has become a "hot" issue for three reasons. First, the Uruguay Round of Multilateral Trade Negotiations under GATT has substantially expanded the normal purview of trade agreements to include, for the first time, trade in investment, services, and IP. The final GATT text requires all signatory states to adopt, within few years of the accord coming into force, an IP system for plants and microorganisms. Governments could include IP for animals if they wish.

Second, the Convention on Biological Diversity itself has stirred considerable debate and some confusion. Policymakers are struggling to find a balance between the North's access to bio-diversity and the South's access to biotechnology. Others regard this "balance" as the juxtaposition of two totally different issues. In the midst of this, the danger of, or the need for, IP protection emerges as a factor in both biodiversity and biotechnology. With the Convention in force as of the end of 1993, there is an urgent need for a common understanding of the role of IP within the Convention. Suddenly, foresters and farmers, environmentalists and economists are trying to find their bearings in IP law, arguably the last and most daunting legal wilderness on the policy landscape.

Although policy- and opinion-makers are driven to their law books by GATT and the Convention, these two most obvious factors tend to obscure a third. The role of new technologies in global and national society is expanding fundamentally. First, the explosion of synthetic fibres three and four decades ago and now the explosion in microelectronics and biotechnologies have pushed the management of innovation and the role of IP into the centre of the commercial stage.

Neither the South nor the North has fully grasped the impli-cations. Society, at large, does not understand the role of innova-tion. Policymakers have not really considered the interaction of extremely diverse technologies with IP law. *Recent IP initiatives have incited both enthusiasm and alarm.* Those in the private and public sectors who are generating the new technologies, and those who are charged with regulating IP, are floating in an uncomfortable and risky policy vacuum. Likewise, indigenous and other rural communities — who have the longest innovative tradition and the largest bio-diversity contribution — carry on without appropriate recognition and compensation. The policy vacuum has led to a number of sometimes alarming, sometimes inviting, patent applications and decisions.

The "Brain" Claim

Perhaps the most notable of the "Brain Claims" was the initiative by the US Government's National Institutes of Health (NIH) to apply for a patent on 2 851 genes and DNA (deoxyribonucleic acid) fragments associated with the human brain. In a single application of more than 1 000 pages, the NIH challenged conventional inter-pretations of the basic IP concepts of "inventive step" and "utility." The US Patent and Trademarks Office has twice rejected the NIH claim for these reasons and noted that it would have taken its examiners until the year 2035 to review the application (Waldholz and Stout 1992). Nevertheless, the NIH initiative stimulated a like application by the British Medical Council and, possibly, by others. The unprecedented move has caused concern even among re-searchers in such fields as distant from human physiology as rice and maize. Many observers breathed a sigh of relief when the NIH announced recently that it would no longer pursue this patent policy. Nevertheless, some worry that a body as influential as the NIH has pointed to an IP path that could see monopoly control over the most important genes in the breeding of food crops. Concern increased in April 1994 when Incyte, a small US biotech concern, revealed that it had indeed taken the NIH lead and applied for a patent on 40 000 human genes and DNA fragments and declared that it would pursue its claims aggressively. This is an issue that will remain controversial in the intellectual property community for some time to come (Fox 1994).

The "Species" Claim

A patent has recently been granted for genetically engineered cotton. The sweeping claim, unless successfully challenged, gives the patent holder a monopoly over all forms of genetically engi-neered cotton, regardless of germplasm or technique. Although the patent was granted in the United States, the claim is pending approval in Central America, China, Europe, and other countries and regions. The patent was also accepted in India — an important cotton-growing country. It may be possible for the applicant to bar transgenic cotton imports into any country recognizing its claim. The patent could profoundly influence the future of a $20 billion crop critical to the economies of many countries of the South. There is a widespread feeling, shared by many in the biotechnology industry, that the cotton claim has overreached the bounds of acceptable patent law. In early 1994, the Indian Government took the unusual step of rescinding the patent claim on the grounds that it was against the best interests of its people.

As the Group was wrapping up this report, it learned of the 2 March 1994 approval of another "species" patent, this time on a food crop. The Soybean species patent granted by the European Patent Office to Agracetus, a wholly owned subsidiary of W.R. Grace Company, has the same implications for this $27 billion food and feed crop as the earlier US Patent Office approval for cotton. In the case of both soybean and cotton, W.R. Grace is the patent holder. The company has advised that it has other patents pending for rice, maize, groundnut, and beans. There is no indication, however, that these other patent applications (current or pending) are "species" patents and some industry observers regard this possibility as unlikely (RAFI 1994a).

The Coloured Cotton Claim

In a neighbouring field of IP known as Plant Breeders' Rights (PBR), a different kind of concern has arisen around certificates granted for two varieties of coloured cotton. Farmers' organizations in Andean countries believe that the varieties are an obvious extension of the original coloured cottons developed in South and Central America by indigenous communities, and the breeder herself confirms that the original seeds were collected in Mexico and Guatemala (RAFI 1993). Here, the concern of the farmers is not (in contrast to the preceding patent cases) that existing laws are being distorted or ignored. Rather, farmers are concerned that the existing law completely fails to recognize their major contribution to the newly developed product — leading to gross unfairness.

The Merck/InBio Initiative

The scene, however, is not one-sided. Although a range of views exist on the merit and risks associated with bilateral arrangements, the contract established between the pharmaceutical company, Merck, and an NGO, InBio, in Costa Rica offers practical recognition of the value of biodiversity to industry. Merck is providing $1.135 million for 10 000 extracts from biological accessions gathered by parataxonomists (Reid 1993). The partners have also agreed on a royalty-sharing system if any of the material is commercialized.

The Shaman Partnership

A second drug company, Shaman Pharmaceuticals, has announced its intention to return a percentage of profits back to all countries and communities it has worked with after any and every product is commercialized. Compensation will be funneled through the Healing Forest Conservancy, a nonprofit organization founded by Shaman for the conservation of biodiversity and the protection of indigenous knowledge. Shaman's research has already led to patent claims and the company accepts that the resulting royalties are based upon not only its own contribution but also that of the communities from whom it has received medicinal plants. The company has developed contracts with some indigenous communities in Latin America but it could be some time before it will be possible to determine the benefit of the arrangement for the communities involved.

Every example cited here has its advocates and opponents. The first general conclusion we are able to draw collectively is that the IP system is in flux; not only the rules of the game but the game itself may be changing as science and society grapple with the marketing of new biomaterials. National opinion- and policymakers are advised to proceed with caution.

Not only the rules of the game — but the game itself — are in flux.

THE PLACE OF INNOVATION

Intellectual property policy should be considered within the wider context of a policy in support of national innovation. Such a policy should bear in mind the need to support and strengthen the innovative role of farmers and indigenous communities. The policy might also consider the role of the formal innovation system of public and private researchers and the potential for cooperation among these three. Too often, research and development (R&D) policies are seen solely in the light of public or private research. The need to stimulate diversity within and among different centres of research has often been overlooked. Most neglected of all has been the creation of opportunities to enable rural communities to collaborate with the formal sector. The dynamism of the community innovation system has been underestimated. Although Agenda 21 speaks long and often about "indigenous knowledge," policymakers are left with the impression that this knowledge has little or no current utility. This is incorrect. The successful development of biological diversity will depend upon the creative relationship that can be nurtured between two opposite poles — formal and community systems. For this to work, policymakers should seek to complement the "transfer of technology" model of development with more participatory approaches to research and extension. True participation means that farmers and rural peoples must exercise practical power and command resources that will facilitate their analysis and support their experimentation. The formal system must respond with professional, institutional, and policy changes that will allow them to listen to and work with communities as equals in research endeavours.

Four approaches are needed. First, new experiments in participatory analysis and joint strategic planning are required. Participatory approaches that support local innovation and adaptation, augment diversity, and enhance local capacities are more likely to generate sustainable development. Second, new learning environments (for both community and formal researchers) are needed to establish the mutual understanding that can lead to negotiated programs that are arrived at jointly. Third, new institutional struc-tures may be necessary to give all parties the freedom to collaborate efficiently. Fourth, new policy frameworks are needed that create stability and confidence within the formal innovation system and, equally, demonstrate a national commitment to the strengthening of rural societies, with a practical recognition of their role in con-servation and development. The extent to which governments and other policymakers can ensure equitable and equal collaboration between community and formal systems will be the extent to which countries benefit from their biodiversity.

> **Recommendation**
>
> **1. The United Nations, through the good offices of the World Intellectual Property Organization (WIPO), should consider con-vening an international conference on society and innovation. This conference could be held in 1998, on the occasion of the 125th anniversary of the Vienna Conference that brought about the international patent system of today.**

THE HUMAN CONTEXT

Ultimately, the reason to conserve plant genetic resources and to encourage innovation in the conservation and development of these resources is to improve the quality of human life. This goal is easily stated and easily forgotten. Because almost any activity can be construed to be for the benefit of humanity — given suffi-cient imagination and long time lines — the only certain way to ensure that innovation serves a useful purpose is to build in the active participation of society in all aspects of the innovation process.

Nowhere is this more true than in the contemplation of sys-tems of IP related to life forms. For a variety of reasons that may not be immediately obvious for everyone or entirely clear to any-one, the notion of IP over living materials evokes strong responses from virtually every quarter. Intellectual property trends in the last few decades have stimulated a remarkable debate in governments, industry, and among academic and indigenous peoples' organizations. From the governments of Canada and Sweden to the corporate offices of Imperial Chemical Industries (ICI) and Ciba-Geigy to the councils of the Guaymi General Congress and the World Council of Churches, an extremely important and energetic debate is underway. It is not likely that this short report can contribute substantively to such a debate. It is important, however, to take the debate seriously.

Within the Crucible Group, some see IP as nothing more than a variation on commodity property rights and, therefore, IP on a plant variety as not substantively different from property ownership over livestock or a harvested crop. As much as most societies allow human beings to exercise life or death power over animals and plants, even to the point of determining their reproductive activity and breeding characteristics, IP over the same creatures does not seem to extend our domination of other life forms any further. In the case of food crops and medicines, it is now perfectly possible, treating these basic needs as a commodity, to withhold them from peoples and whole countries. Governments have withheld foods and medicines for political reasons from time to time. To the extent that excessive pricing can be a barrier to access, some companies could be accused of withholding foods and medicines as well. The Crucible Group would unanimously agree that humanity's basic needs must be met and that it is our global responsibility to make sure that they are met regardless of politics or price. With resolve, the international community can work together to ensure that these needs are met. There is no need to eliminate private property in the process.

Others in the Crucible Group make a distinction between physical ownership over individual biomass, including its products and progeny, and ownership over the products and processes of life itself. For the first time in human history, it is possible to have monopoly ownership over the "formulae" that make life—including the genes and gene complexes that establish characteristics.

The European Patent Office announcement that an application has been filed by researchers at the University of Pennsylvania involving transgenic human sperm and indicating the capacity to select or deselect specific human genes has heightened concern. It now seems possible, with the patent on all forms of transgenic cotton, to lay claim to processes of life across an entire species. Even the successive generations and further invention related to a species might be subject to the original patent. This, some argue, is a qualitatively different issue than mere property ownership.

There are also societies, countries, and cultures to whom the concept of IP itself is foreign. To extend this alien system over living materials can be unthinkable. In many cultures, the Western concept of private property does not exist — or is observed in a more collective manner. Some indigenous communities regard such ownership as outrageous.

When IP is extended to include human living materials, the same communities, and many others, become deeply disturbed. Recent patent claims made on human T-lymphotrophic viruses derived from the immortalized cell lines of indigenous peoples in Panama, Papua New Guinea, and the Solomon Islands have caused alarm and anger. That the human cell-line viruses have been claimed by a foreign government has added to the concern. A similar claim by a Swedish pharmaceutical company of human material taken in Italy has also caused debate.

Surprisingly, it is the patent claim made by the US government on the virus from the human cell line of a Guaymi woman in Panama that brought the ethical debate to both GATT and the Convention on Biological Diversity. In late 1993, the President of the Guaymi General Congress met with GATT officials and determined that human genetic material could be considered to be in the GATT patent provisions then under discussion. Nothing in the adopted text excludes human material. Members of the Guaymi General Congress went on to appeal to the Intergovernmental Conference of the Convention on Biological Diversity that met in October 1993. The Guaymi appealed for protection from patenting under the Convention. The issue, whether human genetic material is within the scope of the Biodiversity Convention or not, is expected to be debated at a forthcoming session of the Contracting Parties (RAFI 1994b). In November 1993, the Guaymi patent application was withdrawn by the US Government. However, the other human cell line claims related to the citizens of Papua New Guinea and the Solomon Islands remain.

Those who oppose IP systems identify a trend that began with the patenting of ornamentals early in this century and moved on, by midcentury, to IP protection for food crops. In the final quarter of the century, the trend spread to microorganisms and animals and, as the world begins Agenda 21, to the species of an entire food crop and the cell lines of human beings. Whether there is real reason for concern or not, the Crucible Group acknowledges the importance of the debate and the need for ethical issues to be addressed by all parties in public fora.

Recommendation

2. **The international community should recognize that some new technologies, and even the concept of IP itself, can pose far-reaching ethical concerns for some people, as well as for whole countries and cultures. These concerns must be honored.**

DIFFERENT VIEWPOINTS

I. THE CAUSES OF GENETIC EROSION

Does IP contribute to genetic erosion — or does the diversification of breeding activity increase genetic diversity?

Viewpoint A — Unacceptable Market Pressures

Although the direct effects of IP on genetic erosion might be tenuous, the indirect effects can be very significant. Intellectual property enhances incentives for commercial plant breeding, shifting efforts inexorably toward the development of varieties with the largest market potential, that is, major crops that are widely adapted across large areas and with characteristics that best meet the needs of commercial farmers and the marketing and processing industries. Crops with less commercial potential that are adapted to specific environmental niches, or that are better suited to the needs of smaller scale farmers, risk being neglected and, as their comparative profitability suffers, may be abandoned. The effects are the same whether IP provides a stimulus to private-sector breeding or forces public-sector research, which is increasingly strapped for funds, to focus its attention on commercial agriculture. As private breeding companies become stronger, pressures are created to reduce public spending on plant breeding and to concentrate instead on basic research for corporate use.

Intellectual property means that seed companies obtain a higher return on protected varieties than on unprotectable traditional varieties. There is a strong tendency to make only minor changes in the market leader and rely on marketing to sell the variety as something really new. Intellectual property establishes a commercial bias in favour of the newest varieties and, to meet the criteria for PBRs, emphasizes physical distinctiveness and uniformity at the expense of significant genetic variability. To this end, IP results in increased genetic uniformity and, where diversity still exists, more genetic erosion.

Viewpoint B — A Minor Factor Worthy of Consideration

There is no evidence that IP is a major cause of crop genetic erosion. There is concern, however, that, unless properly monitored and controlled, the presence of IP can contribute to a market and regulatory environment unfriendly to unprotected commercial seed and farmers' varieties or both. There is, obviously, a greater capacity to manage this concern in rich than in poor countries. Although PBRs' criteria for distinctiveness, uniformity, and stability, combined with the cost and risk of developing new varieties, could bias commercial breeding toward uniformity. It is also probable that, to the extent that IP encourages breeding investment, genetic diversity would be a by-product of more breeding work. It is important to create incentives for breeders to develop specialized varieties, for example, of subsistence crops and those adapted to marginal areas. This might be achieved, for example, through extending the period of protection for such varieties. Perhaps the best insurance is the continued involvement of a strong public-sector breeding effort.

It is commonly stated, although not necessarily proven, that the presence of IP is hampering international germplasm exchange and, hence, access to sources of diversity by breeders. Genebank directors and breeders are possibly more reluctant to "give away" germplasm that might have commercial value. Given developments in GATT and increasing legislative activity on IP in the South, further study, including surveys and empirical data collection, are needed. Meanwhile, the message to policymakers must be to proceed carefully.

Viewpoint C — The Problem is a Lack of Political Diversity

Crop genetic erosion is a serious problem, but IP issues seem connected to this problem largely for political reasons. During 3 years of debate in the Keystone Dialogue process, the only consensus reached on this was that the political turmoil stirred up over IP was causing a constraint in international germplasm exchange and that this constraint could have negative implications for genetic diversity (Keystone Center 1991). A major cause of genetic erosion has been a negative side effect of the introduction of improved varieties from public-sector national and international research programs — varieties that have helped feed an additional 500 million people and that were developed without any influence from IP. Habitat destruction and changes in farming systems are also significant causes of genetic erosion, unconnected to IP.

Far from exacerbating genetic erosion, IP, by increasing investor confidence and offering breeders an opportunity to profit from their work, increases and diversifies the number of breeding institutes and stimulates the development of a wider range of crop varieties. The variety of strong breeding programs also supports genetic diversity by increasing the support for genetic resources conservation as a matter of enlightened self-interest. Changes introduced in the 1991 UPOV convention to discourage breeders from making only small changes to existing varieties also help to increase genetic diversity among released varieties. Broad demographic and agronomic factors have caused genetic erosion. Intellectual property may prove to be one of our best hopes to increase genetic diversity.

II. IP SYSTEMS — ADJUST OR ABORT?

Are IP systems merely adjusting to meet the needs of new biotechnologies — or is IP dangerously out of control?

Viewpoint A — Flexible Mechanisms
Responding to New Challenges

Intellectual property systems have shown themselves to be a highly flexible market mechanism in support of innovation and technology transfer. In the best-known system, patents have adapted, over the past century, to meet the demands of electrical energy and nuclear power. Inventors have moved from steam engines to aerospace on the basis that patents reward usable, nonobvious inventive steps with a temporary commercial monopoly in return for full scientific disclosure and effective social access to the invention. It is no coincidence that the unparalleled expansion of human knowledge over this century has been accompanied by a corresponding evolution in the IP system.

Neither is it surprising that each shift in the technology paradigm requires adjustment within the IP system. As government patent offices retrain and reorganize to interpret the new science, some confusion and discomfort are inevitable. As with other technologies, the new biotechnologies are forging reinterpretations within IP systems. Undoubtedly, some of the patent office decisions have surprised even the inventors who sought their protection. Time, experience, and the marketplace will bring order to the system. Intellectual property is a self-financing mechanism that offers inventors a fair opportunity to recoup their research investment without guaranteeing anyone a profit. The short-lived inventor's "monopoly" only yields profit if the invention itself meets genuine needs — and those who pay the royalties are those who benefit from the invention.

Viewpoint B — Monopolizing the Products
and Processes of Life

In an IP system, governments intervene in the marketplace to create private monopolies over the key engines of technological progress. Since the formation of the IP system 120 years ago, the original social "contract" has been reworked six times. On each occasion, the monopoly privileges of industry have strengthened and the rights of society have weakened. Were patents merely to ensure an opportunity for inventors to obtain a return on their investment, there would be little debate. Today, however, companies demand exclusive monopolies allowing them not only royalties but to set the conditions for access to their inventions. In a global marketplace, international companies can use IP systems to cross-licence one another in different regions and even in different industries thus allowing them to erect barriers to the entry of new companies and countries. Under the patent system, technological power goes to those with the largest legal departments and deepest pockets.

With new biotechnologies, corporations are attempting to extend control to that 45% of the world economy based on biological products and processes. We are witnessing the ungainly spectacle of companies trying to take the patent system designed for machines and make it work with plants and animals instead. The result includes successful patent claims on entire plant species like cotton, on animals, and on parts of the human brain. This is not a self-correcting mechanism. This is an attempt to gain exclusive monopoly over the very nature of life.

Viewpoint C — Systems in Need of Help

Intellectual Property systems represent a kind of contract between society and inventors and their investors. As with any such arrangement, both parties must monitor the balance of benefits and obligations to ensure that technological progress continues and that society's needs are answered. The application of the industrial patent system to biological processes and products is stimulating unprecedented debate; in the social context, as some question the appropriateness of patenting life forms; in the technical context, where there is concern that patents may be an inefficient method of protecting new biotechnologies; and, at the political level, where corporate and sovereign nation interests are juxtaposed.

Whatever one's view of the patent system, some recent biotechnology-related patent claims provide a legitimate cause for concern. It is clearly more difficult to establish consistent technical criteria and to determine an equitable inventor–society balance for the application of IP systems to living resources than it is for inanimate objects. As with the protection of copyright, computer software, or integrated circuits in semiconductors, it may be useful to consider a *sui generis* system of IP for biotechnology. Such a system should take into account the inherent complexities of applying IP systems to life forms, the contribution of many generations of local communities in shaping those life forms, and the need to balance the interest of society as a whole for continuous innovation with the interest of the individual inventor for reward and compensation.

2. PLANTS

THE NEW FRAMEWORK FOR
BIOLOGICAL DIVERSITY

Some 40% of the world's market economy is based upon biological products and processes (Gadbow and Richards 1990). In the rural communities of Africa, Asia, and Latin America, where the majority of the world's people live, the dependence on biomaterial can run to over 90% of human survival requirements. In an increasingly urbanized world, it is difficult for those of us inside city gates to remember that more than half of the food humanity consumes is bred and produced by the people who eat it, and that 8 out of 10 members of the human family turn to community healers and medicinal plants for protection from illness (Joyce 1992).

Although the Crucible Group fully recognizes that the protection of species and ecosystems is a powerful moral obligation, we also know that any sound conservation strategy must correspond with the interests of the people who depend upon diversity most immediately. Conservation programs that meet the needs of these people have a good chance of working, and we ignore this fact at our peril. Artificial barriers between conservation and sustainable utilization must be broken down. Rural communities use diversity because they need to. To them, diversity means choices and opportunities. Acknowledged and empowered, rural communities are arguably the most effective, efficient, and economic conservers of biological diversity.

Conservation programs that meet the needs of those who depend upon diversity have a good chance of working. We ignore this fact at our peril.

PLANT GENETIC EROSION

The biomaterials most important to local communities must form the basis for any conservation and development strategy. First and foremost are food crops and livestock breeds. The wild relatives of domesticated species are also essential. Plants that produce medicines, fuels, clothing, shelter, or meet cultural needs are no less important. Most of these essential parts of biological diversity are most readily conserved within their own ecosystems. This hard fact offers policymakers an unambiguous starting point for their work.

It is from this perspective that we place so much importance on plant genetic resources. This is where the developmental and the environmental agendas come together. To develop (and even commercialize) crop and medicinal plants, the widest possible range of genetic material must be available. However, the genetic diversity of our critical plant species is disappearing at a terrible pace. The foundations of our biomaterials security is eroding.

The reasons for crop genetic erosion are many. The importance of many of the reasons is contested. Nevertheless, one basic biological reality remains. In the world's most critical food crops, seed is not only the means of production, it is also the end product for consumption. Without proper conservation, the replacement of one crop with another or of a farmers' variety with a semidwarf variety, for example, can mean that the discarded genetic material is eaten. A hundred generations of farmer-bred diversity can disappear in a morning pot of porridge.

A hundred generations of farmer-bred diversity can disappear in a morning pot of porridge.

When farmers look to distant markets to sell their surplus crop, they often sow different, more commercially viable varieties. Government regulations or farm credit schemes sometimes force the adoption of specific plant varieties or even whole new crops. In other cases, farm communities enthusiastically adopt what they regard to be improved seeds. In any of these cases, commercial agriculture tends to increase genetic uniformity and this, in turn, leads to genetic erosion. Intellectual property systems (patents and PBR) encourage commercial agriculture and may accelerate genetic erosion. Biotechnology research focuses on commercial agriculture and leads to demands for IP protection with the same potentially negative consequences for genetic diversity.

Whatever the continuing causes of genetic erosion, the fact remains that the best efforts of farmers and scientists have not slowed the pace of gene loss. Despite the signing of the Convention on Biological Diversity in Rio, a genuine global commitment to the safeguarding of this most valuable resource still seems far away.

NATIONAL CONSERVATION STRATEGIES

Whether a policymaker's starting point is ecological sustainability, food security, or trade enhancement, a key step in any national strategy is to secure biological diversity as the resource base for innovation. The primacy of national strategies for genetic resources can be defended on the political grounds of sovereignty and, equally, on the practical grounds that this is the economically least expensive and socially most functional approach. As the Crucible Group understands it, biodiversity is most useful at the national level. Domestic programs will generally be the first to benefit from strong conservation strategies.

Conventional wisdom has argued that germplasm can best be stored through temperature- and humidity-controlled facilities and through field genebanks linked to ongoing research programs in the biosciences. Although we fully endorse this approach, we see it as only one part of a more sophisticated and participatory endeavour.

The impact of genetic erosion is felt differently by different research systems. For the institutional (or "formal") innovation system, genetic erosion is felt when breeding material is not readily available in genebanks. For the community (or "informal") innovation system, the loss is felt when breeding stock is no longer found in the field or in local markets. It is only a small consolation to either system to know that the other system may still retain the breeding material within their own technological borders.

Herein lies an important distinction. Despite the good will of all parties, there continues to exist a barrier denying farmers access to conventional genebanks. Conversely, in-field erosion spells the end of formal-system collection efforts and imposes a ceiling on the contributions of commercial plant breeders.

This barrier can be overcome wherever a sense of justice and equity prevails. Obviously, the informal system continues to contribute bountifully to the stockpile of seeds finding their way into genebanks. Likewise, genebanks have repatriated rice to farmers in Cambodia and Sri Lanka and maize and sorghum to Somalia when wars and famine have left communities without their customary breeding stocks.

However, except for a highly innovative initiative among farmers, NGOs, and the Government of Ethiopia, known as the Seeds of Survival Programme, a systematic and equitable gene flow between the two systems is virtually unheard of. There are two reasons for this. First, until recently, the practical conservation and real plant-breeding contribution of local communities was not understood by the formal sector. Second, insufficient seed-source information, incomplete collections, or a lack of infrastructure for seed multiplication and distribution often make it difficult or impossible for genebanks to replenish farmer losses.

Farmers, therefore, have access to their "banked" material only theoretically. In reality, farmers may never see this material again and may or may not have access to improved germplasm based upon their material. The innovation "ceiling" for informal breeders lowers immediately and finally when they become solely dependent on seed bred by other

For farmers, plant extinction can take place when seed leaves the field. That it is stored in a genebank is no guarantee that they will ever see it — or its progeny — again.

people in other places and, sometimes, for other purposes. Governments and companies, although they may desire otherwise, can rarely guarantee direct access to banks, cannot (in these difficult economic times) guarantee that the genebank itself will survive, and cannot promise that improved breeding stock will find its way back to the farm community. Put bluntly, many, maybe even most farmers, cannot always rely upon the formal innovation system to replenish seed from lost community varieties.

With respect to crop seed and other plant germplasm amenable to *ex situ* storage, a national conservation program should be built on the principle that multiple strategies are essential.

> *The Ethiopian approach to on-farm conservation merits consideration by other countries.*

Community germplasm maintenance, including "community genebanks," should have high priority. National genebanks are a second level of assurance. Further backup, and an alternative storage possibility for countries without genebanks, can be to ensure the deposit of seeds in international facilities and the facilities of other nations that guarantee treatment in ways acceptable to the local communities and the nation. We strongly endorse this principle.

Rather than repeat work that has been done elsewhere, we commend the final consensus report of the Keystone International Dialogue on Plant Genetic Resources, adopted in Oslo in June 1991. The Keystone Report (Keystone Center 1991) offers a very helpful summary of the major institutional, financial, political, and scientific issues related to both national and international conservation efforts.

Farmers and local healers have a tremendous wealth of knowledge and practical experience that is invaluable. Communities can provide an early warning system for the disappearance of species and for genetic erosion. Community members can improve the quality and speed the pace of characterization and documentation. With outside support, resources can be conserved and research can be extended.

Although the Crucible Group strongly endorses the closest possible collaboration between community and institutional sectors, we also acknowledge that there can be political, social, and economic obstacles to this cooperation that spring from issues far wider than conservation itself. There can be very legitimate grounds for mistrust. The international community should not attempt artificially to impose cooperative strategies in regions and countries where this is not realistic. Nevertheless, recognizing the long-term importance of biodiversity to human survival, informal and formal systems should work diligently to overcome these barriers.

Recommendations

3. Each country should formulate a specific national action plan for the conservation and use of plant genetic resources, within the framework of a wider strategy for the conservation of biological diversity. Such an action plan should seek out all opportunities for constructive collaboration among scientists, policymakers, and rural communities, both within the country and beyond national borders, with regional and international initiatives.

4. The Crucible Group recommends that genebanks reconsider their policies for collection, storage, and distribution to ensure that they are compatible with the FAO Code of Conduct for Germplasm Collection and Exchange. National and international genebanks can be responsible partners with the informal system when they are prepared to collaborate with farmers' organizations and indigenous communities as equals and with the same access and opportunities they afford to other institutions.

INTERNATIONAL STRATEGIES

In the period from the early 1970s to the early 1980s, at a time when the new, high-yielding varieties were rapidly replacing local varieties in many parts of the South, there was growing concern that an irreplaceable resource was being lost and that concerted efforts were needed at the international level to conserve this resource.

During this period, the International Board for Plant Genetic Resources (IBPGR) was created by the CGIAR with a secretariat within FAO. Also during this time, the FAO Commission on Plant Genetic Resources was established as an intergovernmental policy forum. Major efforts were made to collect materials from farmers' fields and to secure adequate storage. Although the materials collected were predominantly from the South, many of the materials came to be housed in genebanks in the North — in part because of the facilities that existed in the industrialized countries and partly for political reasons. In the mid-1970s, there were only 10 countries with national germplasm conservation programs — 15 years later, more than 100 countries had strategies (IPGRI 1993).

Although FAO's involvement in genetic resources dates back several decades, it was in 1983 that member governments established the International Undertaking on Plant Genetic Resources — a nonbinding agreement to cooperate in the conservation of genetic material and to work together for its sustainable development. The initial Undertaking was later modified to recognize both Plant Breeders' Rights and Farmers' Rights. Although the FAO initiative continues to speak of plant genetic resources as a common human heritage, this moral and somewhat theoretical construct has been submerged in the more immediate political premise that nations hold sovereign right over the genetic resources within their borders. The Undertaking also laid the foundations for an international funding mechanism and for the establishment of the FAO Global System including a Network of Ex-Situ Base Collections, a Global Database, and a full program and plan of action. Partly for financial reasons and partly because of the preparatory work leading to the Earth Summit and Agenda 21, much of the practical work in the FAO initiative remains to be enacted.

During the 1980s, IBPGR (now the International Plant Genetic Resources Institute, IPGRI) attempted to establish an international network of *ex situ* base collections for the conservation of crop germplasm. In total, 219 storage agreements were reached. At the beginning of the 1990s, IBPGR merged its network with that of

FAO. The legal status of much of the germplasm transferred as part of this network remains to be fully resolved. Slightly more than half of all the 219 agreements were with genebanks in the North. The remainder were divided almost equally between genebanks in the South and those of the international agricultural research centres (IARCs) (1993 IPGRI data).

Despite these significant efforts, it is clear that much more remains to be done. Although much genetic variation within major food crops has been collected, there are still many species that have not been adequately conserved and that remain under serious threat of erosion. In addition, materials already housed in gene-banks cannot always be regarded as secure. Inadequate facilities, lack of funding, and human-resource constraints combine to make the system a very uncertain foundation on which to base future agriculture. If the situation is still unreliable for conventional seed-producing species, it is much more so for those crops that have to be conserved vegetatively — in field genebanks or in *in vitro* collections. For such species, much research must be done just to develop appropriate conservation technologies.

Also, efforts to conserve genetic diversity at the local level have largely been overlooked. With concern for the ability of genebanks to conserve adequately the genetic variation needed now and tomorrow, and with the new awareness that farmers themselves are the primary managers of germplasm, there is an incentive to work together. The intergovernmental community must recognize the rights of farmers over their biological heritage and must provide appropriate incentive systems to enable them to continue to develop it.

It is unreasonable to expect all countries to be fully self-sufficient in respect to the conservation and improvement of their genetic resources. Collaboration on a regional or international basis provides a way in which each country can meet its own needs in a cost-effective manner.

The imperative to conserve genetic resources *in situ*, both on-farm and in the "wild," has brought many new actors, including

NGOs, onto the international stage. They have brought with them a wide range of perspectives. Some come essentially from an ecological conservation perspective, whereas others put genetic diversity conservation in the context of the need for the empowerment of rural communities. All concur on the need to develop mutually supporting systems that will ensure that plant germplasm will be effectively conserved.

The Convention on the Conservation of Biological Diversity attempts to provide a legally binding framework for such a system. As yet, however, for reasons discussed in the following section, it remains an imperfect — or at least incomplete — instrument.

THE CONVENTION ON BIOLOGICAL DIVERSITY

On 29 December 1993, a broad and legally binding Convention on Biological Diversity came into force. With that step, the Biodiversity Convention became the most important initiative ever taken to set the world on a course toward environmentally sustainable development. The Convention is a global instrument committing signatory nations to work in common cause. This is its central value and message. The Convention also supports national sovereignty and the right of countries to benefit from their bioresources. It further highlights the right of countries to have access to technologies, including new biotechnologies, that could assist the conservation effort or that may have use in the exploitation of biological resources. Together, these common decisions represent an essential first step on a long road toward new global and national conservation programs.

The Crucible Group is concerned, however, that the unique role of agricultural biodiversity is not well understood in the Convention. This fact is evident from the unresolved issues identified in Resolution Three of the Nairobi Final Act (22 May 1992). The resolution noted that both Farmers' Rights and the status of collections made before the Convention (mostly *ex situ* crop germplasm) need more debate. Some of the implications and options are discussed in the following sections.

The Problem of *Ex Situ* Collections

The exclusion of genebank and botanic-garden material collected before the coming into force of the Convention poses a difficult problem. Some members of the Crucible Group believe the effect is that, unless this issue is resolved satisfactorily, almost all of the biomaterial that we know to exist and that is most likely to be commercialized in coming decades is unprotected outside of the Convention and beyond the reach of countries in the South who were the major donors. By this analysis, the Convention only applies to that material that we do not know to exist and that will probably not be commercialized in the foreseeable future. Unless otherwise established through agreed interpretations to the Convention, this new legal covenant, for the first time, acknowledges the right of governments and corporations that obtained the South's germplasm before the Convention to declare this material their own and to control access to it and benefit from it. If this is the case, some members contend that the Biodiversity Convention of 1992 could become the biggest "rip-off" of indigenous peoples, and of their knowledge and materials, since 1492.

Other Crucible Group members recognize the Convention's limitation but insist that any "retroactive" measures would fly in the face of normal legal practice and, more important, be unworkable. Some surveys have shown that 65% of the material in genebanks lack basic passport or characterization data (Lyman 1984). National sovereignty could not be applied. The monumental task of assigning and proportioning value over old collections, further, would probably not yield significant benefit to donor countries. Tracing the genetic path of commercial crop varieties and drugs to assign retroactive value could prove

If the Convention safeguards only material that we do not know to exist and do not know to have value, it could become the biggest "rip-off" since 1492.

technically unrealistic and only create new disputes where the world requires cooperation. The Convention, with all its failings, affords the international community a new beginning.

Successful implementation of the Convention will require a framework to facilitate appropriate technology and germplasm transfers for the mutual benefit of all interested parties. It should provide clear and unambiguous policies on germplasm and technology exchange. The frameworks should:

- Promote partnerships in the equitable sharing of both responsibilities and benefits at the community, national, and international levels;

- Enable appropriate codes of conduct to be formulated and implemented;

- Promote conservation and sustainable use of biodiversity; and

- Develop a specific protocol to address the special needs of agricultural biodiversity building upon the history and experience of the FAO Commission on Plant Genetic Resources.

Farmers' Rights

Aside from the uncertainty regarding the status of *ex situ* collections, the other outstanding issue identified by governments is that of Farmers' Rights. First espoused at the founding meeting of the FAO Commission on Plant Genetic Resources in 1985, Farmers' Rights were incorporated into an annex to the FAO Undertaking. Resolution Three of the Nairobi Final Act, confirming the text of the Biodiversity Convention, notes the importance of Farmers' Rights and calls upon governments to consider its incorporation into the Convention itself. The Earth Summit in Rio also recognized Farmers' Rights and the concept appears in Agenda 21.

We are aware of a two-way transfer of technology. Indigenous and other rural-community knowledge and technology of relevance to biomaterials and the ecosystem is important. It gives those in the formal sector who acquire it opportunities for commercialization. One of the most important and most difficult issues facing the Convention will be to recognize and economically valuate indigenous knowledge and find a way to give substance to Farmers' Rights.

This issue is all the more important because it is usually juxtaposed with Plant Breeders' Rights. Some supporters of Farmers' Rights contend that it is immoral to allow Plant Breeders' Rights over commercial crop varieties unless the international community also accepts Farmers' Rights over the crop varieties they have bred for their own

Is the Convention a "fast GATT" for IP proponents, or a sidetrack for opponents to pirate private research?

fields. This view has sometimes led policymakers to equate Farmers' Rights with IP and to assume that it is simply another word for the monopolization of plant varieties. The original advocates of Farmers' Rights — South and North — insist that Farmers' Rights is not, and could never be, considered as an effort to claim monopoly control over living materials. By recognizing Farmers' Rights, society acknowledges the historic and continuing role of farmers and indigenous rural communities in creating, maintaining, and enhancing biological diversity.

In our view, the model developed by the Keystone International Dialogue on Plant Genetic Resources should be considered. This model proposes the creation of a sustained international fund, provided for by governments via the standard United Nations' formula, and administered through a United Nations' agency governed on the basis of one nation–one vote. The fund would be directed through a scientific and technical advisory committee to programs and projects that would encourage regional, national, and community conservation and germplasm enhancement. The fund would not attempt to assign benefit for the commercial use of farmers' varieties to individual countries or farmers. The Keystone Dialogue suggested a fund of not less than $300 million per year over the life of Agenda 21.

At a meeting in Madras in early 1994, the Government of India indicated its willingness to give substance to Farmers' Rights for its rural citizens through the taxation of seed industry profits. Some national seed companies within India have also expressed their willingness to surrender a percentage of their royalty returns from Plant Breeders' Rights to farm and community organizations. In an informal proposal for farmers' rights legislation arising from the Madras Meeting, participants recommended that 5% of the gross income from the sale of seeds of new varieties be returned to rural innovators (Swaminathan and Hoon 1994). Other companies — some international — do not believe that a direct charge to their industry is fair or appropriate. If brought into law, this will be the first time that any country has legally acknowledged Farmers' Rights. That the Government may adopt both Farmers' Rights and Plant Breeders' Rights in the same legislation will fuel the fires of debate from New Delhi to Geneva. The Indian initiative will become an important precedent for other countries.

For industrialized countries, IP rights remain the key outstanding consideration with respect to the Biodiversity Convention. The United States initially refused to sign the Convention for this reason. Many companies, and some governments, see the ambiguous language in the agreement as an opportunity for the South to usurp their innovations and to avoid adopting IP legislation of their own.

Yet another industry view argues that the Convention makes it legally correct for companies to regard improved biomaterials as their own property and, thus, under the universal terms of the Convention, to require that all others wishing access to this material agree to any financial or other conditions laid down by companies. If this is the case, the argument runs, then the Biodiversity Convention goes beyond GATT in entrenching an IP system for biomaterials (Deusing 1992). Various governments have drafted "agreed interpretations" that they hope will be considered by the Contracting Parties to the Convention. The intent of each draft is to clarify this very confusing and uncomfortable situation.

The issues of germplasm collections assembled before the Convention, the conditions of access to genetic resources, and the practical recognition of Farmers' Rights remain to be negotiated. It is essential that agreement be reached on such issues — and quickly. The further development of a truly effective global system for the conservation and use of plant genetic resources — which involves all actors at the local, national, regional, and international levels, private and public — depends on such agreement.

Over the next few years, FAO is expected to play a lead role, in close association with the Biodiversity Convention, in resolving these issues. Ultimately, agreements are expected to be formalized as a protocol to the Convention. FAO plans, in 1996, to hold the Fourth International Technical Conference on Plant Genetic Resources, at which the structure, role, and strategy of the future Global System will be articulated. The process of negotiations leading to the conference is expected to result in two major documents — the State of the World's Plant Genetic Resources and the Global Plan of Action on Plant Genetic Resources. Together these will provide a blueprint for the future.

Recommendations

5. To date, the international funding community has failed to recognize fully the seriousness of the loss of plant genetic resources in farmers' fields and in genebanks. The Crucible Group recommends that any new funding mechanisms arising from the Biodiversity Convention or other global forums allocate specific funds for the conservation and sustainable development of on-farm, *in situ*, and *ex situ* collections of plant genetic resources.

6. The Crucible Group recommends that the issue of the status of *ex situ* collections obtained before the Convention be a major item for resolution at an early meeting of Contracting Parties.

7. The Crucible Group cannot offer a common interpretation of Farmers' Rights or the intellectual property aspects of the Convention. We do urge, however, that every effort be expended to resolve this issue to allow the international community to truly set about the task of safeguarding the world's invaluable flora and fauna.

(continued)

> **Recommendations**
>
> 8. The Crucible Group commends the Fourth International Technical Conference on Plant Genetic Resources, scheduled to take place in 1996, as the most appropriate process for the resolution of all of these issues. It is essential that all concerned parties become actively involved. The Group calls especially upon those who negotiate these important agreements to take into account the role and importance of community-based efforts. The Technical Conference may prove to offer the best process for the full definition and implementation of Farmers' Rights.

DIFFERENT VIEWPOINTS

III. IP FOR FARMERS

If there is a general recognition that the role of farmers in plant breeding is underestimated, is it either possible or advisable to develop or modify an IP system that will meet their needs?

Viewpoint A — Not Monopoly Rights: Farmers' Rights

The setting for innovation in indigenous communities is aimed at personal and free community application. Innovation in the industrialized setting is for personal application and for charging for the use by others of even those within the community. When these two systems meet, it is within the nature of both that innovations communally applied in the indigenous sector will be privatized by the industrialized sector. Because it is the industrialized sector, which is mostly in the North, that is making a commodity out of otherwise free goods, the onus is on it to take the substantive moves to correct the injustice.

Both Breeders' Rights and patents can be adjusted to offer protection to community innovation. Farmers' varieties are much more genetically variable than breeders' varieties. Environmentally speaking, this is a strength, not a weakness. It is true, however, that it makes varietal identification more difficult for scientists of the industrialized sector. Indigenous farmers, however, have systems of recognizing and naming their own varieties, and these systems could be given legal recognition. As for patenting, the system can already accommodate traits, whether the genes determining these traits have been identified or not. Patents could, therefore, be granted to some specific farmers' varieties and to medicinal and other useful plants within the existing norms of the industrial sector. Alternatively, a new *sui generis* legislation, perhaps inspired by the Unesco model legislation on folklore, could be developed for indigenous communities. All that is required is good will by the industrial sector to recognize the innovative, but largely unmonetized and thus weak, indigenous sector, represented by its community organizations and not by individuals as innovators.

Viewpoint B — First: A Multilateral Funding Mechanism

The range of IP options available to farmers and indigenous peoples has not been fully explored. It is worthwhile to examine every opportunity. Specifically, FAO, Unesco, UPOV, and WIPO might be asked to convene an international meeting of experts to explore this issue in conjunction with industry, NGOs, and farmers' organizations. Only rarely, however, has a farmer's variety been commercialized even in neighbouring countries — much less totally different ecoregional zones. It is equally rare to find whole plants used in developing new pharmaceutical products, and local healers seldom have a chemist's knowledge of the active compounds important to patented medicines. Thus, it is unlikely that further study will yield an IP avenue that is both legally and realistically useful.

The Convention on Biological Diversity, or a protocol for Agricultural Biodiversity, can best respond to the need for IP protection of rural societies through an assured intergovernmental funding mechanism administered on the basis of one nation–one vote and directed to the practical support of specific programs and projects intended to bring about rural development and to conserve and enhance plant diversity. This mechanism should be part of the Global Initiative for the Security and Sustainable Use of Plant Genetic Resources as recommended in the Final Plenary of the Keystone (Oslo) Report.

Viewpoint C — Supporting Innovation
Where It is Known to Occur

On the one hand, even though it is true that innovation takes place in communities, its speed is slow and it cannot be attributed to specific individuals. The individuals who contribute toward it do so in the process of doing work they see as productive, and not in a deliberate innovative act. For this reason, the innovations are fortuitous and freely available. That is why germplasm, even agricultural biodiversity, is a common human heritage.

On the other hand, modern innovators search for a problem felt by society, and specifically design an innovative act to solve this societal problem. For this reason, society should compensate them. They invest considerable sums in the expectation that it will. The IP rights system is aimed at doing this. This system should be strengthened if society wants an acceleration of innovation to solve its mounting problems with biodiversity and its utilization.

The question may arise as to what the benefits would be for indigenous communities, whose innovation, whether intended to be an innovation or not, is being used as raw material by the modern innovator. When the crops that an indigenous farmer grows are improved by the innovator, those same communities would benefit from improved yields and increased production. When an obscure traditional medicine is turned into a drug with world-wide availability, access to it is assured even in its indigenous setting. The effectiveness of all this would reduce if the IP of the innovator is not protected.

IV. THE CONVENTION ON BIOLOGICAL DIVERSITY

Did the world take a major step forward with the signing of the Convention on Biological Diversity — or did we put our best foot in our mouth?

Viewpoint A — One Step Forward: Two Steps Back

The Convention has excluded existing *ex situ* collections from being governed by its provisions. Through the Convention, therefore, the world has decided to safeguard all the germplasm that we do not know to exist or to have value while committing all that we know exists and is likely to have value to commercial application. At least two-thirds of all collected germplasm is in institutions held or dominated by the North. Most of this germplasm comes from the South.

To cap it all, the Convention recognizes the IP systems of the North, which are aimed at encouraging commercialization by the private sector. However, it fails to make any provisions to balance this by compensating the local communities, mostly of the South, who have created much of the germplasm and all of the indigenous knowledge on Southern biodiversity. The Convention perfunctorily recognizes their contribution and stipulates that the application of IP systems should be supportive of its provisions. Even this is considered excessive by some Northern governments that are now, it seems, getting ready to craft interpretive statements to this effect when they ratify the Convention. The good news is that the Convention language is loose enough to allow the South to fight for interpretations advantageous to it, including the creation of a special protocol on Biodiversity for Food and Agriculture as proposed in FAO.

Viewpoint B — Out-of-Step: But Forward Nevertheless

The Convention on Biological Diversity lays out the scientific and organizational principles and framework for a global conservation strategy. It also announces an international political commitment to biodiversity protection and enhancement. This is no small accomplishment in an era of economic restraint. It will take further negotiation, the experience of practical cooperation, and continued good will to surmount these challenges.

As indicated by its accompanying resolutions, the Convention needs to address the special problem of *ex situ* collections and Farmers' Rights. FAO's proposal to establish a protocol for Biodiversity for Food and Agriculture under a revised International Undertaking may at least partially resolve these issues. The proposed International Technical Conference on Plant Genetic Resources, with its accompanying State of the World Report and Global Plan of Action, may be a good process for negotiating them. Finally, the continuing uncertainty about a biodiversity funding mechanism and its operation has stimulated a number of bilateral negotiations. Although this could prove helpful, more probably the net result of bilateral agreements will disadvantage smaller countries and bias global conservation efforts and priorities.

Viewpoint C — Side-Stepping the Tough Realities

The Convention on Biological Diversity is an undeniable triumph of international commitment and good will. Unfortunately, the clock ran out in both Nairobi and Rio before the exercise could be completed. Missing is an unambiguous statement affirming that most new technology is generated by (and is the property of) private researchers who cannot be forced to surrender their rights.

In the presence of such ambiguity, it is difficult for industry to commit itself fully to the Convention. The ambiguity destabilizes investor, and inventor, confidence in the feasibility of innovative research and jeopardizes the world community's capacity to work with biological diversity at a time when this work is most sorely needed.

The private sector's concerns are exacerbated by some of the debate that has arisen since Rio, hinting that the Convention should become uniquely "retroactive" and that some kind of inter-governmental discipline must be asserted against the mutually negotiated and beneficial agreements of sovereign governments and companies. The Contracting Parties should act quickly to remove the uncertainty. The Rio process succeeded in strengthening private-sector support for biodiversity. With the uncertainties set aside, governments can and will discover a strong new ally in private research.

3. PEOPLE

DIVERSIFYING THE INNOVATION FRAMEWORK

We cannot conserve the world's biological diversity unless we also nurture the human diversity that protects and develops it. We need diversity in the innovation processes related to biomaterials. Policymakers must find a way to stimulate innovation at the community, national, and international levels — in formal and informal, public and private sectors. The challenge of Agenda 21 is to find equitable mechanisms that allow these diverse forms of innovation to collaborate for the benefit of humanity.

COMMUNITY INNOVATION

In the aftermath of the Rio Earth Summit, the contribution of indigenous and rural communities as innovators has been recognized but not necessarily understood. That indigenous peoples inhabit the most diverse fields and forests of the world is sometimes viewed as both coincidental and unfortunate. That a correlation could exist between the uses made by people of biological diversity and the availability of that diversity is seldom considered.

Obviously, much of the innovative activity of farmers lies in their fields. The Mende farmers of Sierra Leone, independent of foreign experts, conduct field trials, test new seeds against different soil types, and compare results (Davies and Richards 1991). In the Horn of Africa, Ethiopian farmers maintain variety performance records, sometimes inscribed on door posts. Farmers normally breed for specific microenvironments, but it is often the case that their folk varieties can perform remarkably well in roughly similar environments in other parts of the world. Research institutes report the use of an Ethiopian farmer variety in Burkina Faso, and of a

South African variety released in Ethiopia. Rural societies maintain agricultural biodiversity because it is essential to their survival. They breed their own improved varieties for the same reason. There is no useful distinction, for them, between conservation and development.

Minimizing risk is an important part of the livelihood strategies of rural communities. West Africa's Azande farmers actually increase both the number and the complexity of their crop experiments following poor harvests (AAS 1989). Faced with striga weed infestation in their millet, farmers in Niger have sought out advice from other Sahelian communities with longer experience and developed strategies to "trap" striga by interplanting sesame (Yates 1989). From cassava cultivators in the Dominican Republic to potato growers in the Andes and rice farmers in the Philippines, formal sector researchers are now looking for, and finding, genuine inventiveness.

Institute-based agricultural scientists, however, still predominantly male, may find rural innovators especially hard to find because many of them (some say most) are women. Sudanese farmers–breeders are usually women. Kayapo women in the Brazilian Amazon not only breed new crop varieties but preserve representative samples in hillside genebanks (Smith 1985). Tanimuka and Yukuma women in the Colombian Amazon have bred and preserved numerous clones of peach palm with spineless trunks and unusually large and seedless fruits. During the 1984 famine in the southern Sudan, Toposa women risked their own lives to hide the seeds for the next year's planting (Berg et al. 1991).

However, the cultivated fields and the domesticated crops are just one part of the story. In fact, evidence is mounting that virtually all of the biodiversity within the reach of rural communities — be it in the fields or in the forests — has been nurtured or developed by community conservers and innovators. What we have often called "wild" species may be more properly called "associated" species as they are often an integrated part of farming systems and can be considered to form part of the intellectual achievements and contributions of rural societies. The Chacoba of Bolivia, for example, make use of almost four-fifths of the woody species in their surrounding forests. The Ka'apor of Brazil use three-quarters of their tree diversity, whereas, in Venezuela, the Panere use about half their documented diversity. All of them use between one-fifth and one-half of all woody species for food and up to one-third for medicinal purposes (Prance et al. 1987).

The importance of so-called wild species to the food supply of rural communities is brought home by the Mende of Sierra Leone who draw less than one-fifth of their nutrition from cultivated species and more than half from forests, streams, and fallow fields. The remainder comes from local markets and plantation crops (AAS 1989). In the Bungoma District of western Kenya, almost half of all families incorporate wild species in their home gardens and only a marginally lower percentage of families collect them for food in the forests (Juma 1989). Because local communities rely on foods collected throughout their environment, distinctions between the biodiversity in agricultural and natural ecosystems are blurred. The maintenance of diversity in all ecosystems is important to meet the twin goals of conservation and livelihood security.

Despite their importance for livelihood security, these crops of local importance, farmer-developed varieties, and wild foods are largely ignored by conventional agricultural and forestry R&D that focuses attention on a limited number of domesticated crops of global importance. Policymakers should ensure that new agricultural technologies and changing patterns of land use and land tenure do not reduce the availability of wild food resources, or eliminate the use of local crops and varieties. On the contrary, appropriate policy incentives are needed to support the conservation and sustainable use of this important part of agricultural biodiversity.

The Application of Farmers' Rights

Agenda 21 endorses an FAO concept known as "Farmers' Rights." This concept, adopted by all FAO member states recognizes the dynamic seed-improvement capabilities of individuals and their communities. Farmers' Rights was originally seen, at least in part, as a counter-proposition to Plant Breeders' Rights and, in part, as an international funding mechanism to compensate farmers for their role in conserving and improving germplasm. Since its conceptualization, Farmers' Rights has come to describe the whole spectrum of requirements that, ideally, makes plant genetic resources (PGR) a true resource.

First, for the best use to be made of PGR, farmers must first control their own biomaterials and have access to as wide a gene pool as possible. Second, farmers are entitled to retain and control their own knowledge about genetic resources and to access knowledge and information about their material when it is available elsewhere. Third, farmers need funds and financial support to develop their resources. A fourth necessary component is the capacity building for farmers to develop further their own technologies and to make appropriate use of, and adapt, other technologies. Fifth, farmers must have the freedom to control and develop their own farming systems. This includes their right to land and access to markets — in essence, the freedom to determine their own way of life. These five elements transform genetic materials into genetic resources.

Community innovation requires:
  Germplasm
  Information
  Funds
  Technologies
  Systems

Capacity building is central to this view of Farmers' Rights. Farmers and rural societies must be supported by governments and international institutions in their effort to continue to generate and conserve PGR and to improve their own well-being. Policies should be implemented that will create an environment conducive to the empowerment of local communities and a partnership between institutional and community-based researchers. This means ensuring that local communities are full participants in the definition of national and international R&D priorities. Both Keystone and FAO have called for the creation of a sustained funding facility established within the framework of the United Nations, guided on the basis of one nation–one vote and directed to the support of programs and projects that will strengthen community conservation and innovation.

The Crucible Group noted the concern of many farmers and policymakers in the South who believe that some forms of IP could make it illegal for farmers to sell seed to their neighbours or even to save seed for the next planting season. This issue is addressed in a later chapter.

Another concern relates to the question of equitable benefit. As argued earlier, the contribution of rural innovators to the institutional and the commercial sectors is substantial. At the time of the Earth Summit, the NIH launched, with the US Agency for International Development (USAID), a "drug discovery" project in the South. The strategy is to make use of "the wealth of knowledge held by traditional cultures." Similarly, the Shaman Pharmaceuticals company has pioneered new approaches to work with rural communities that seem to be bearing commercial fruit. A cooperative agreement has been made, for example, with the Consejo Aguaruna y Huambisa in Peru. About half of the 400 species collected by the company have shown some medicinal potential and two drugs are now in clinical trials. Shaman's discovery costs are one-tenth of the cost of traditional laboratory techniques. By working with community innovators, the efficiency of screening plants for medical properties has improved by more than 400% (Daes 1993).

There are many instances where the innovative technologies of rural communities have been lost, without benefit, to others. In the 1970s, Micmaq fishing communities on the Canadian East Coast applied their knowledge of the marine ecosystem to an oyster problem. The Micmaq technology was immediately copied by industrial operators with access to financial markets and the community not only did not profit from their technology but lost some of the local industry to outsiders (Daes 1993). In the same way, Amazonian communities have watched their R&D on the peach palm be exploited by institutional innovators without either recognition or compensation. With an impressive protein yield and adaptability, the peach palm may come into wide use in tropical areas, but there are no indications that the economic gain resulting from it will be shared with those who have nurtured and developed it for centuries.

In this context, the concern of rural societies and indigenous communities to benefit from and protect their intellectual achievements should not be surprising and, in fact, should be encouraged by formal-sector innovators. The Crucible Group recognizes the continuing contribution of community innovation systems to agriculture, medicine, and other fields. The Group also agrees that current systems of IP protection either do not address the inventive process of the informal system or, for economic and technical reasons, are inaccessible to rural innovators. Current IP systems do not provide incentives to innovations generated at the community level. This leads to both inequity and distortion. The IP system can be distorted to allow others to acquire indigenous technologies without appropriate acknowledgement or compensation. National innovation policies — and international conventions — should address this unacceptable inequity.

Recommendations

9. Innovation strategies should promote decentralization, diversity, and democracy within local, national, and international communities rather than promoting excessive centralization, uniformity, and control.

10. Current IP systems do not provide incentives to innovations generated at the community level. Any innovation policy adopted at the national or international level should take this into account.

NATIONAL (PUBLIC AND PRIVATE) INNOVATION

National development plans should include strategies to stimulate agricultural and other rural-based innovation. Traditionally, national innovation strategies have emphasized the formation of a network of public research institutes. All too often, biomaterial institutes including genebanks, botanical gardens, cell libraries, and plant breeding facilities have been treated as second-class centres. In the new environmental and economic equation of the 1990s, a strong research capacity in all the biosciences, especially for the South, is just good sense. The creative challenge for science-policy managers today is to build equitable relationships with informal innovators and the private (for-profit) sector.

These are difficult bridges to build and even harder for some of us to cross. With government cutbacks on research funding (despite increased awareness of the need for research) and with shifting global political philosophies, governments have come to rely more heavily on the private sector to meet at least part of the research agenda. It is tempting to envision a trilateral relationship of equal research partners involving public and corporate researchers and community innovators. Yet the reward systems and social "pay-offs" for different researchers are likely to be different as well. Incentive systems must be taken into account in drafting innovation strategies.

For many countries, this has resulted in pressures to adopt IP legislation and to establish other incentive and regulatory mechanisms that attempt to ensure that private research is at least consis-

> *A national program that does not seek to exploit the creative role of the private sector could be imposing its own internal "brain drain."*

tent with national priorities. Such mechanisms may or may not be fully effective. There is also a need in many countries to evaluate them and to look for additional ways in which the private sector can contribute.

The private sector, including pharmaceutical and seed companies, has a genuine interest in the conservation and development of biological diversity. There is full awareness that not only long-term environmental security but also the well-being of their own enterprises and of their customers rests upon the sustainable use of the widest possible range of biomaterials. Few companies, however, can afford to invest in long-term conservation. The pressure to produce also means that commercial enterprise can seldom risk the investment needed to work with "exotic" germplasm or to explore new species. This economic fact pushes the functional utility of uncharted biological diversity (that not catalogued and characterized in genebanks or gardens) well into the future — and well out of practical consideration. Companies do not debate the importance of diversity, but they have no realistic means by which they can incorporate its conservation into their plans and budgets. Nevertheless, companies are generally highly supportive of governmental and nongovernmental initiatives to conserve diversity and willingly work to encourage governments to allocate additional financial resources for this purpose.

National innovation strategies for plant genetic resources could consider exploring additional roles for the private sector. For example, the introduction of a new crop or variety by a company could well meet the development needs of farmers and society but might also result in the extinction of farmer-bred varieties. In such instances, companies, as responsible social institutions, could be expected to advise authorities in time for the biomaterials to be conserved. The private sector could also play a front-line role, along with informal innovators, in an "early warning system" to monitor changes in agricultural practices and habitats that could cause genetic erosion.

Countries and communities that do not encourage the full participation of all the (formal and informal) inventive human genius within their borders imperil their own progress. The conservation and enhancement of biodiversity, in fact, play to the two great strengths of the South. The South has the greatest biological diversity and the greatest stock of human genius in the use of their diversity. The critical challenge is not how to monopolize innovation but how to bring about cooperation between the two broad systems of innovation and between public and private innovators. The world cannot afford the luxury of barriers, cutting off the ideas of one from the ideas of the other. The conservation and sustainable development of biological diversity demands the formation of a new covenant under which herbalists, farmers, laboratory scientists, universities, cooperatives, and corporations can work together for the well-being of humanity.

Such lofty words cannot mask the fundamental power imbalances and risks involved in bringing diverse systems together. The Crucible Group strongly advocates the creation of a new research covenant within each nation, but it stresses that such covenants must ensure mutual respect and mutual benefit. The covenant must also guarantee each party intellectual independence and strengthen the capacity of each for self-reliance. It is to be expected that some countries will not be able to meet these important criteria, and genuine collaboration will not be possible.

Governments and rural societies need to work together to establish feasible mechanisms to allow farmers and herbalists to help other researchers and administrators understand rural

> *Strategists need to support research relevant to the needs of communities that involves local crops and local markets.*

realities. Governments can encourage the development of new enterprises in a number of ways. Private initiatives (including cooperatives) may get underway by providing conventional agricultural services, such as seed cleaning and produce transport. From this base, they could develop a local research capacity. International enterprises could also play a role in national research. Most developing countries, however, do not provide a sufficiently affluent and consistent market to attract international seed companies. Corporate breeding programs generally target specific crops with varieties designed for relatively large, well-defined markets and special growing conditions. These conditions are more likely to be found in temperate climates, although they occur elsewhere. It is usually a case of serendipity when a variety bred for an intended large growing area can also meet unique local needs. For this reason too, strategists need to consider how best to support research relevant to the needs of communities that will not be a profitable market — and for commodities that are not of global interest.

The Crucible Group believes that the encouragement of small, innovative service and research enterprises is an important step toward a healthy national strategy. A range of incentives from tax breaks and subsidies to support for higher education and rural infrastructure should all be considered as part of this strategy. Furthermore, the Group believes that, for many countries in the South, it is possible to encourage innovation in the private sector without IP protection.

Recommendations

11. The decision of whether or not to adopt some form of IP protection for plant genetic resources should be taken within the framework of wider national strategies to promote science, innovation, and conservation.

12. A national strategy in support of innovation should, as one of its primary objectives, create an environment in which community innovation systems and formal (public and private) research institutions receive fair recognition and equitable reward for their contributions. Such a strategy should nourish a climate of cooperation among all innovators.

13. Although the Crucible Group has differing opinions on the role of international companies, there is general agreement that, along with rural innovators and universities, local entrepreneurship as expressed in the form of cooperatives, companies, and other intiatives could be broadly beneficial and is worthy of serious consideration.

4. PATENTS

DIVERSITY ALTERNATIVES WITHIN THE GLOBAL TRADING SYSTEM

GATT AND AGRICULTURAL BIODIVERSITY

The Uruguay Round of negotiations, which concluded on 15 April 1994 in Morocco, under the rules of GATT have been a focus in IP discussions since talks began in 1986. Operating on the assumption that the famous Dunkel Draft Text would ultimately be adopted, the Crucible Group debated its merits throughout 1993 and reviewed our conclusions in the early months of 1994.

Our report does not address the entire 26 000-page GATT agreement nor all of its implications for either agriculture or the environment. We do review the Trade-Related Intellectual Property (TRIPS) text in the overall accord for its possible effect on biodiversity. In this context, the Group notes that, for the first time in GATT, IP is seen as a trade topic. With the adoption of the latest agreement, signatory states are obliged to adopt a patent system for microorganisms and to establish either patents or some *sui generis* form of IP for plants. It is left open to governments whether they would also patent animals. One possible mechanism to implement a *sui generis* system of protection for plant varieties, is the Plant Breeders' Rights system offered by UPOV. Established in 1961, UPOV operates under the umbrella of WIPO and has 24 member states signatory to its 1978 or 1991 Conventions.

The term *sui generis*, however, may offer a wider range of policy choices because it could, presumably, include any arrangement for plant varieties that offers recognition to innovators — with or without monetary benefit or monopoly control.

Article 27:2 in the new trade agreement allows countries to exclude from patentability any inventions whose applications are seen to cause "serious prejudice to the environment." To the extent that IP could adversely affect plant genetic diversity by accelerating genetic erosion, this environmental clause may enable countries to restrict or avoid patent protection on plants. The applicability of this clause is disputed however, as it might be difficult (or impossible) to prove the intricate relationships between patents and genetic erosion in court. Some Crucible Group members, therefore, recommend that the TRIPS text be supported by an "Agreed Interpretation" allowing countries to apply Article 27:2 to exclude IP on plants and parts thereof if they find it useful in conserving biological diversity.

The Crucible Group has intensely differing views on the place of IP in trade agreements and, in particular, on the impact of such systems on living materials. These are outlined in the following sections.

More surprising than the differences within the group, however, are the similarities. With respect to GATT–TRIPS, the Crucible Group agrees on the following points:

- No country should be coerced into adopting an IP system for living materials. There are valid ethical and practical reasons why each country should be allowed to reach its own position and either adopt an existing mechanism for protection, create a new mechanism better suited to national interests, or encourage innovation by other means altogether.

- Existing conventions for IP protection favour those with ready access to economic and legal resources and can work unfairly against those who do not have such access.

- Current IP conventions are not designed to acknowledge the intellectual contribution of informal innovators. This omission is one reason why the intellectual "stock" of these peoples and of developing countries is undervalued. The absence of such acknowledgment has led to the unquestioned and unchallenged appropriation of the innovations of rural communities.

- The encouragement of commercial plant breeding through IP rights can be beneficial to countries and to farmers. It can, however, also work to the detriment of small-scale farmers and could, for example, lead to a further loss of genetic diversity in the field and could be administered in such a way as to constrain farmer-based plant breeding. If this is the case, proper policies and appropriate administrative systems have to be put into place to avoid these and other implications.

Recommendations

14. Sovereign states cannot be required to adopt systems of IP in areas that risk the well-being of their peoples or that jeopardize the biological diversity within their borders. Neither should countries be expected to adopt unrealistic time frames to enact IP provisions related to international trade agreements.

15. Any potential conflict between IP proposals and other intiatives for plant genetic resource conservation and exchange should be taken fully into account in interpreting responses to the GATT agreement.

The Patent Option

Within the range of options being offered to cover plant varieties under GATT–TRIPS, the best known is the patent system. It has become increasingly possible, and increasingly attractive, for commercial breeders of crop varieties and for pharmaceutical houses to use patents to protect their inventions.

The Crucible Group has predictably differing views on patents and, in particular, on patents on living materials. Those who oppose the patent system, approach the issue from several perspectives. Some believe strongly that it is ethically improper and practically damaging to allow IP control over life forms. Still other opponents argue that IP systems must be recognized as nothing more than state-created private monopolies and that the system is intentionally scale-biased in favour of the large and powerful against the small and vulnerable. This latter group believes that IP systems control and, therefore, deter innovation and award power over technological development to the enterprise with the largest legal staff and deepest pockets. Developing countries, they argue, be it Switzerland and the United States in the last century or Brazil and Thailand in this century, have developed most quickly when their right to tap human knowledge is unrestricted by artificial monopoly. Historically, countries that have not been the leaders in the development of new technologies have either emphasized the right of their citizens to have free access to inventions without patents or have granted preferential national treatment so that their access to foreign technology is unfettered. Once these same countries establish their own technology base, they often turn around and demand of less-developed countries the restrictions that would have made their own progress impossible.

Opposition to IP on ethical grounds arises largely from the concept of ownership over living products and life processes including the regeneration of life (note our earlier discussion on the "human context"). These opponents note a fundamental difference from the transfer of ownership of seeds or specific animal breeds without any claim on their progeny. This involves owning biomass only, and is a practice as old as commerce itself. The retention of rights over the regenerative capacity of organisms, while selling their biomass, is entirely new and extends ownership beyond society's accepted limits.

Among those who oppose the patent system for economic or ethical reasons are those who would argue that IP is inappropriate when it attempts to encompass the basic necessities of life. They contend that our daily bread, or bowl of rice, should not be the subject of a private monopoly. If nothing else, the world's essential food crops and medicines should remain outside of the patent field.

Yet others detect a contradiction between the argument that plant genetic resources (including genetic information) in the form of farmers' varieties should be made fully and freely available as a common heritage of humankind and the claim that plant genetic resources, adapted through commercial breeding, can be exclusively monopolized. The world would benefit by the free availability of all technological materials and information. Failing this, equity requires that farmers' varieties enjoy comparable protection to those of commercial breeders.

Other members of the Crucible Group consider the foregoing views unrealistic. Supporters of IP see this form of protection as both a human right and a social necessity. As individuals have the right to protect their personal possessions and property, inventors have the right to protect their ideas from being exploited by others who have contributed nothing to their development. In their opinion, patents defend the individual inventor and small company from predatory business practices that would usurp their contributions. Businesses invest money in developing new inventions. Only some are successful. If these can be immediately copied freely, innovators cannot recover their development costs and go out of business. Society loses the benefit of the innovations they would otherwise have made.

Proponents of IP understand protection to be particularly necessary for biological materials, such as plant varieties where others can effectively multiply or "photocopy" the work of several years in a single field over one growing season. Proponents regard this as unjust but, more important, as a fundamental constraint to innovation. Neither creative individuals nor research investors can afford to commit major resources to work that can be so readily usurped. A condition for a company to invest in research is that it can foresee circumstances in which it will recover its investment. The concept of IP is a critical building block in turning the benefits of modern science into products people can use. As we prepare to enter the 21st century, it is hardly surprising that inventors in biological sciences seek to use the tools that made enormous gains in physical sciences possible in the 20th century.

Despite its wide differences of approach, the Crucible Group can easily see a number of practical market reasons why private enterprise, in particular, would prefer patents to other IP systems. The Group agrees, however, that, for conventional plant breeding, such as still dominates in both industrialized and developing countries, there is no necessity to adopt the patent model as the sole method for protecting plant varieties.

Although the foregoing is a general conclusion, some members of the Group see adoption of PBR under UPOV as a constructive alternative to patents. Others regard the UPOV system as only the lesser of two evils that will still, inevitably, push countries in the direction of the patent system.

It is difficult to judge the appropriateness of the patent system, especially for South countries, when that system is undergoing so much change. The advent of new biotechnologies has both in- creased the significance of the patent system

There is no need for the South to adopt a patent system for plants.

and added to a climate of uncertainty sur- rounding its purpose and effectiveness. In recent times, the patent system has "spun off" new approaches to IP. The global com- puter software industry ($43 billion in sales in 1990), for example, seeks IP protection under copyright law in most countries (van Wijk and Junne 1992). In a related field, 19 countries have enacted *sui generis* IP laws for the integrated circuits (or semiconductor "chip") industry. These laws are a hybrid between standard patent law and copyright protection, offering inventors more flexibility than patents but less control than is normally granted by copyright (van Wijk and Junne 1992).

Some countries adopted *sui generis* patent legislation for plants earlier in this century. Although roughly similar to industrial pat- ents, plant patent laws were modified to meet the particular needs of breeders. The formation of UPOV three decades ago was another attempt to create an international industry-specific solution to a protection problem. Their target then, as it remains today, was not to encourage the breeding of food crops but to safeguard new kinds of flowers and ornamentals. Roses and chrysanthemums continue to be the most commonly protected plant species (Figure 2).

For patents to be granted, their application must include a full written description of the invention and how to carry it out. Patents on biological materials have been criticized by some for not fully disclosing necessary details to enable the invention to be successfully repeated. The very nature of life forms makes such a full description impossible. Some argue that "life" patents run counter to the very rules of the patent system in which it is assumed that an inventor gets a patent in return for a full disclosure of the invention. Proponents of the system deny that this is a major problem, but fully agree that invention concealment, where it occurs, is unacceptable.

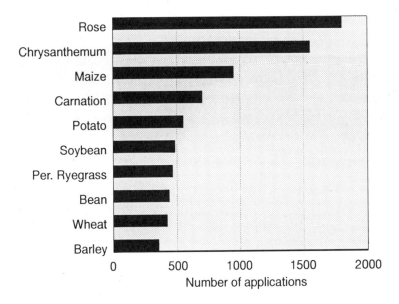

Figure 2. The most protected plant species: PBR cerficates applied for in the six most active UPOV member states as of 1991 (adapted from UPOV 1991a).

Defenders of the patent system within the Group are in full agreement that patents on biological processes and products should meet all the normal requirements for patentability. This includes proper disclosure. Others, however, feel that adequate disclosure is factually impossible and that the new biotechnologies collectively warrant their own *sui generis* legislation. An international system created almost 125 years ago to patent machines and factory parts may not be the best system for plants, animals, and microorganisms.

Patent examiners are undoubtedly having difficulty adjusting to the new biotechnologies. This may be why there is wide-spread uncertainty in the plant-breeding, pharmaceutical, and other industries over life-form patents.

Biotechnology may warrant its own sui generis *IP system.*

More than most others, the patent application made by the NIH and Incyte Corporation to claim thousands of DNA segments and two species claims by a W.R. Grace subsidiary over any cotton using any form of genetic modification technique has left many strong advocates of patents surprised and disturbed. The NIH–Incyte application relates to genes of which the purpose and functioning is not at all clear, and the claims of the cotton and soybean patents are so broad that an entire research area (genetically engineered cotton and soybean) can be monopolized by one inventor.

Yet another concern shared by both opponents and many proponents is the recent trend toward patent approvals for plant characteristics not necessarily linked to specific genes. For example, Lubrizol claimed patent rights over the high oleic acid characteristic in sunflowers and advised competitor firms in the oilseed-breeding field that any other high oleic acid invention would encroach on the Lubrizol claim (Wrage 1994). The effect of such sweeping claims can be to discourage investment and innovation in the same broad area by other researchers. Applied in this way, the patent system blocks innovation and competition — exactly the opposite of the purpose of the system.

Many patent proponents believe that the current uncertainty within the system is temporary and that strong traditions and practices will prevail to ensure that patents serve the best interests of inventors and of society. Many others, both supporters and opponents, wonder if it is not time for society to intervene to clarify the system and ensure that the "bargain" between inventors and society is fair and manageable.

The Crucible Group is clearly not in a position to advocate that countries adopt patents on plants. Nevertheless, some

Is the patent system self-correcting, or does society need to take a hand?

feel there could be conditions under which plant patents might prove useful. For example, an export ornamentals industry might well thrive with patent protection. If some indigenous communities are able to either directly protect properties of a medicinal plant or strike a favourable royalty-bearing arrangement with a pharmaceutical enterprise, the benefits could prove substantial.

Although acknowledging the potential for benefit in specific situations, patent opponents believe that such examples are usually flawed exceptions to the rule. The net effect of patents on foreign-exchange transfers, they maintain, will be negative. It is hard to accept that incoming foreign royalties on carnations will exceed outgoing royalty payments for food crops and pharmaceuticals.

Cautions expressed by some Group members with respect to the current patent climate generally apply most to the situation facing the South. Some members are more confident that the experience of the industrialized countries is such that any short-term difficulties will be overcome. For the South, however, the entire Crucible Group was able to offer several specific observations for policymakers who give this option serious consideration.

- As stated previously, national governments must be free to make their own decision regarding patents without external compulsion. A decision on patents must flow from national needs and national innovation strategies and fit within the social and ethical framework of the country.

- Developing-country governments may wish to delay any patent law over life forms until the current ambiguities and uncertainties are resolved, either through treaty changes or court decisions in industrialized countries.

- Only governments with strong judicial systems should contemplate patent protection. Registration and litigation will be demanding and resource consuming.

- Countries adopting a patent system related to living materials must be prepared to divert human and financial resources toward the development of a patent office with specialist skills in biomaterials. In some countries, this could draw funds and talent away from other nationally important priorities.

- Although it is possible to apply for worldwide patents, it is not possible to defend such patents other than country-by-country. Because most countries of the South will be unable to defend their claims themselves, they will need either powerful financial help or a strong partner to whom they will licence their patents so that they can be defended in various countries. All else being equal, licencing arrangements may not yield as profitable a return as direct exploitation; thus, in some situations, licencing may be a realistic if not optimal choice.

- The research exemption, guaranteed under patent law, protects the right of scientific workers to use patented inventions without charge or prejudice for noncommercial investigations. This exemption must be unambiguously secured so that science can be pursued without fear of litigation. Some researchers now worry that patent courts could order an end to their investigations.

Recommendations

16. The research exemption provided in IP legislation ought to be clarified so that innovative research can be conducted without excessive fear of litigation.

17. The Group wishes to advise that both government supervision and the legal enforcement of IP with respect to genes require careful consideration. IP protection for genes is made especially complex because it is sometimes impossible to control the flow of genes between plant populations.

THE UPOV OPTION

As with patents, and for similar reasons, the system known either as Plant Breeders' Rights or Plant Variety Protection (PVP) is undergoing change. The Union for the Protection of New Varieties of Plants (UPOV) offers governments two models of a *sui generis* system for plant varieties. Presumably, states signing the GATT accord will have a choice of either adopting the 1978 provisions or those of the 1991 Convention. There are significant differences.

The Two UPOVs

Under UPOV 1978, governments may select the range of plant species eligible for protection. The right of farmers to replant and exchange the seed of protected varieties is also reasonably secure. Some breeders, however, believe that the flexibility in the 1978 convention is detrimental to commercial breeding. This has stimulated their interest in utility patents for plants instead of Breeders' Rights. Some observers note a regulatory progression, since the forming of UPOV, that continuously strengthens the interests of commercial breeders and that can undermine the interests of farmers. They believe that countries adopting UPOV 1978 will find themselves on a political and policy treadmill leading inevitably to

UPOV 1991 and then onward until UPOV is indistinguishable from the most monopolistic elements of the utility patent system.

Supporters of UPOV regard the juxtaposition of breeders' and farmers' interests as a false antithesis. They see the two as having major interests in common. Under the UPOV revisions adopted in 1991, for example, signatory states are obliged to permit protection for all plant species and kinds. It can be argued that this wider scope encourages innova-

Breeders will not prosper unless farmers do. Strong Breeders' Rights could increase diversity and farmer security.

tion and biological diversity, because breeders can investigate minor crops or bring whole new species into cultivation with the assurance that their work can be protected. The increased period of protection with UPOV 1991, and the general strengthening of rights, also encourages companies to venture into more fundamental research with farther profit horizons and greater risks. This can only benefit farmers, supporters reason.

Genetic Distancing of Varieties

Some breeders are experiencing uncertainties with respect to major provisions in the 1991 convention. One is the functional and legal application of the term "essentially derived" when describing the relation of one plant variety to another. Customarily, breeders work with commercially proven plant varieties to develop a more refined and improved variety. Under the UPOV 1991 agreement, a new variety that is "essentially derived" from a single earlier variety, although eligible for protection, is subject to the existing right on ("dependent on") the earlier variety. What "genetic distance" between the new variety and its predecessor will suffice to make the later variety independent, is a matter for debate, however. Most commercial varieties trace their lineage to other commercially developed varieties. This legal uncertainty is distressing some plant breeders.

Farmer-Saved Seed

Another area of concern, already mentioned, relates to the age-old right of farmers to save seed from one growing season for planting in the next. Farmers have also historically maintained the right to barter or sell seed to neighbours. Under the provisions of UPOV 1991, the rights to replant protected cultivars are removed unless individual governments reinstate them. In such instances, governments are expected to continue to respect the breeder's interests as far as is possible.

Recommendations

18. Although some members of the Crucible Group can identify circumstances where adherence to UPOV 1991 might be immediately beneficial to a developing country, there is general agreement that the 1978 UPOV Convention is less demanding, and would be preferable for some countries for this reason. Governments may, of course, also adopt *sui generis* national legislation that may be similar to UPOV 1978 without the obligation of becoming a member state of the UPOV Convention.

19. Countries should review the operation of national lists of recommended varieties, Common Catalogues of approved varieties, and all other regulations and policies that could constrain the availability of seeds to farmers. Particularly in combination with IP laws, such rigid policies can have a devastating effect on crop diversity by limiting the freedom of farmers to grow traditional as well as new varieties.

SUI GENERIS POSSIBILITIES

One conclusion arising from the Keystone International Dialogue on Plant Genetic Resources (1988–91) was the acknowledgment that, if GATT–TRIPS were adopted, the only IP in the world that would not be protected would be that of indigenous communities. With these words, the Keystone report identified a fundamental inequity in the current IP system.

To deal with this inequity, there are three (possibly comple-
mentary) choices: to develop a *sui generis* system of "protection"
that will meet the letter, if not the spirit, of the GATT proposals; to
propose mechanisms that will protect the intellectual achievements of indigenous peoples and rural communities within the IP
system; or to propose an alternative *sui generis* system of intellectual recognition that may be outside of IP protection. The Crucible
Group explored each of these options.

Alternative Licence Approaches

Yet another course might be to adopt a system of compulsory
licencing or of Plant Breeders' Rights on Living Organisms. "Compulsory" licencing, or related forms of "automatic" licencing, has
been the subject of hot debate
throughout the entire history of
international IP conventions.
Under an automatic licencing
regime, national legislation re-
quires that inventors make their invention available to all those
prepared to pay. Under other legislation, compulsory licences may
be awarded by patent tribunals if the inventor fails to make the
invention adequately available to society.

*Intellectual property systems that do
not make space for informal innovators
are fundamentally inequitable.*

Either approach maintains the right of the patent holder to
charge royalties for the use of the invention and, presumably,
allows inventors to seek a fair return on the research investment.
Simultaneously, under a strong
automatic or compulsory licencing system, society is assured of
reasonable access to new discoveries. The global dispute over
these alternative licencing approaches turns on one's view of the
purpose of IP protection and on society's comfort level with private
monopolies. The main objection of private industry to compulsory
licencing is that it reduces control over the use of the invention and
interferes with arrangements for exploitation. Restricted use,

*Would there be support for an IP
system without exclusive monopoly
provisions?*

however, is a concern of opponents of patent protection over living organisms. There may be some basis for compromise, although not one that the Group is able to endorse unanimously.

Protection Within the IP Framework

There is little doubt that countries of the South could apply for patents, PBR, or both covering medicinal plants and crop varieties that would win acceptance under either existing or slightly modified IP systems. With exceptions, however, the short-term economic benefits of such protection would be sparse in most situations most of the time. Furthermore, the adoption of the current model of IP could divert attention and energy from other initiatives.

Some members of the Crucible Group — with other members dissenting — think it worthwhile to consider instituting Community IP Rights (CIPR). Indeed, the proposition arising in Madras that the Government of India

> *Community Intellectual Property Rights (CIPR) with public defenders, gene-tracking databases, and review mechanisms could bring some support to the informal system.*

simultaneously adopt PBR and Farmers' Rights may amount to a form of community IP protection. The implementation of CIPR would require much thought and a careful crafting of legislation. Some Crucible members believe that the task could prove either insurmountable or a waste of human resources. To draw effective benefit from Northern breeders as well as commercial interests in the South, CIPR would require both appropriate national legislation and reciprocal recognition in other countries. Some members believe, however, that an effective system should also include an international database to trace germplasm. A further improvement might be an internationally recognized office for a "Public Defender" to intervene in the potentially unequal relationships that could arise between communities and governments, on the one hand, and between countries and international corporations on the other. The specifics of this three-way interactive system involving national and international legislation and the public defender's role would have to be worked out carefully. These might include, among others, the following four considerations:

- Biomaterial inventions should be deposited for legal record in genebanks or cell libraries together with registration data on the date, place, and environment of origin. The registration reference should also include the names and addresses of individuals and communities who supplied the biomaterial or information related to it. The same information should be attached to all IP applications. Failure to disclose such information should be grounds for refusal or cancellation of the IP.

- Biomaterial currently held in genebanks should be covered by such legislation. Where inadequate registration data make it impossible to do so, such material and materials derived from it should be freely available and barred from IP protection.

- Each national IP office and the international secretariat for each IP convention should create an office to investigate complaints by indigenous communities and governments. A tribunal should have the power to revoke IP in breach of these requirements. The work of the office should be reported regularly.

- Fees from IPs should be used to fund this office and to give legal aid to indigenous communities involved in disputes.

Some members of the Crucible Group regard the suggestions made here as a natural extension of the current work of the IP system. These proposals need not constitute an unacceptable burden on that system. It is current practice for patent offices to assign the full cost of their offices to the fee structure imposed on applicants. The cost of these suggestions, therefore, would simply become an additional part of the "cost of doing business" in the IP community.

Still other members of the Crucible Group, although sympathetic to the need to encourage new forms of innovation at the community level, consider these proposals to be little more than a large administrative burden on the backs of overworked and underfunded genebanks, especially in the South, and a further bureaucratic constraint on the process of innovation for both private and public researchers in the formal sector.

Alternative IP Mechanisms

Provision is made in TRIPS for signatory states to adopt *sui generis* forms of IP protection covering plant varieties. Many policymakers outside the IP field are not aware that IP systems include a number of options that do not imply exclusive monopoly control over inventions. Among these are Inventors' Certificates that can discard financial compensation altogether in favour of nonmonetary awards, and nonexclusive licencing arrangements. There is a great opportunity for innovation in this field. Developing countries, in particular, may wish to explore some of these possibilities closely.

Model Provisions for Folklore

One such possibility is the 1985 WIPO–Unesco Model Provisions on Folklore, which has the benefit of being accepted by both WIPO and Unesco (Unesco 1985). The Model Provisions have three unique elements that are especially appropriate to the protection of biological products and processes.

- "Communities" (rather than identified individuals) can be the legally registered innovators and can either act on their own behalf or be represented by the state.

- Community innovations are not necessarily fixed and finalized but can be ongoing or evolutionary and still be protected by IP law.

- Beyond standard patent or even copyright provisions, communities retain exclusive control over their folklore innovations for as long as the community continues to innovate.

The Model Provisions are not directly applicable to all community innovation. Scientific inventions are specifically excluded, for example. Standard IP law in many countries, however, has expressly or by implication excluded protection for plants, animals, pharmaceuticals, and chemicals. Nevertheless, patent offices and legislators in such countries have often chosen to interpret or change the law to permit the patenting of such innovations, on the assumption that the exclusions have become unnecessary or outdated. (It is said "If the lawmakers had known then what we know now, they never would have made the exclusion.") Certainly, the same case can be made for community innovation systems.

The significant point is that the Model Provisions acknowledge the concept of ongoing indigenous community innovation. It is very unclear, however, whether this offers an effective means of safeguarding community innovations, scientific or aesthetic, or whether markets may be found that could use the innovations. It has only infrequently been adopted in national legislation, and little information is available about how it works in practice. Nevertheless, it might be worth exploring the Model Provisions further.

The WIPO–Unesco Folklore Provisions could give communities monopoly over their evolutionary biological inventions forever.

Material Transfer Agreements

Among other forms of *sui generis* initiatives that might be considered are Material Transfer Agreements (MTAs). This form of bilateral agreement may or may not provide for IP protection, but MTAs do offer possibilities for agreement on how materials will be treated and how any rewards will be shared. Essentially, the material to be transferred is treated as a commodity rather than as knowledge, and a contract is reached between "buyer" and "seller" based on the potential value of the commodity. Such contracts may involve both initial "up-front" payments and then a formula for additional benefit if and when the material is commercialized.

Some members of the Crucible Group believe that MTAs, outside of a more encompassing and collective IP framework, will simply legitimize an unequal situation. For an example of this view, and a contrary position, see the viewpoint box on the Merck–InBio contract. There is a concern that MTAs can be drafted that entrench a more complete monopoly than is now possible under patent law.

Varieties bred by farmers and local communities will rarely conform to standards of distinctiveness and uniformity required by established legal systems. Yet these varieties, in many cases, serve the needs of those who bred and continue to breed them as well or better than those from the formal sector. To develop mechanisms to protect them, new concepts as well as methods for characterization must be devised if rights are to be established unambiguously.

The Crucible Group consistently returned to one of our central themes — that national priorities must drive any decision as to what, or if, IP systems are required in

There has been a distressing lack of innovative thinking about Innovation Systems.

support of innovation. There has been a distressing lack of inventiveness in encouraging innovation. It is possible for a country, for example, to develop a *sui generis* IP system that varies the years of protection depending upon the species involved (as UPOV does), or excludes certain species (for example, some or all basic food crops). Sui generis national laws could vary the scope of protection for different biomaterial categories such as medicinal plants and food crops. The application criteria could also be adjustable depending upon the purpose of the invention or even its origin. It might also be possible to establish unique rules covering national treatment, national working, licencing provisions (compulsory or automatic licences), or a system that discriminates in its fee structure on the basis of nation of origin.

In contemplating options that discriminate in the treatment of nationals and inventors from other countries, policymakers should refer to the overall intent of the GATT Uruguay Round, which is to remove such discriminatory practices.

In reviewing its own discussions on IP, the Crucible Group agrees that neither industrialized countries nor international companies regard the South as a prime target for TRIPS provisions related to biomaterials. With some exceptions, developing countries are not perceived to be a significant market for biological inventions developed in the North; until they are, they will not be any threat to the stability of the patent system. In a sense, developing countries have been caught up in a market debate that is not yet relevant for them. With this in mind, these same countries should not feel pressured to adopt laws or practices that may subvert their national self-interest. The GATT accord makes it possible for South governments to move at their own pace. Formal review of TRIPS enforcement will not take place until at least 4 years after the entry into force of the agreement — or probably not before 1999. Least developed countries can anticipate a further 10 to 20 years within which to respond to these provisions. At the rate IP systems are changing, countries reluctant to adopt new laws now have little reason to hurry.

To illustrate the market focus related to plant variety protection, it is worth noting that three-quarters of all the applications made for plant protection among 24 countries in 1990 involved only six countries. More significantly, more than 60% of all variety applications took place, and more than 85% of all their applications circulated, among these six countries (UPOV 1991a). The interest of these countries in applying for PBR certificates in Africa, Asia, and Latin America seems very remote.

Recommendations

20. Under the principle of national sovereignty, countries should be free of externally imposed requirements to adopt any IP arrangement affecting plant genetic resources. Countries are free to develop alternative (non-IP) or additional approaches for the stimulation of innovations that are best suited to their particular needs, capacities, and opportunities.

(continued)

Recommendations

21. Although the Group finds an assortment of new ideas related to *sui generis* legislation — or amendments to current IP systems — interesting to explore, it cannot reach a consensus on their value. Some feel that the initiatives posed here would prove economically useless and could lead to other forms of exclusive monopoly detrimental to the South and to farmers. Others believe that such proposals that would render current IP system unworkable. We can only recommend that policymakers consider exploring this field.

22. Governments and institutions responsible for plant genetic resources accessions (often held in genebanks) could explore the possibility of filing a "Defensive Publication," as is permitted in the USA. This approach could make it harder for such germplasm to be patented. It may be possible to make one filing to cover the entire contents of a genebank supported by a computer printout of the accessions list.

23. Both bilateral and multilateral agreements have an important role to play in conservation and exchange. The multilateral system, however, needs to be developed further to ensure fairness and coherence. Bilateral agreements should be constructed so as not to jeopardize a strong and harmonious multilateral environment.

24. The Group recommends that MTAs be studied further and be considered seriously by policymakers seeking more flexible approaches to IP systems and compensation for their biomaterials. MTAs would operate most usefully within an international legal framework that ensures greater equity.

25. The Group recommends that governments take advantage of the several years available to them to develop the best possible strategic response to GATT–TRIPS.

THE SPECIAL CASE OF INTERNATIONAL CENTRES

The Crucible Group acknowledges that the IARCs of the CGIAR are faced with particularly difficult choices with respect to IP. The IARCs are responsible for an enormously important collection of genetic material gathered from farmers' fields as well as from public and private research institutes. The mission of each IARC is to work on behalf of small-scale farmers to increase world food security. The IARCs have benefited by the full and free exchange of plant genetic resources worldwide. IARCs provide large quantities of material to bona fide breeders (private and public) in virtually every country on earth. It is their belief that to continue this practice is in the best interest of all nations.

The IARCs' seed-distribution policies have been guided by an international approach to the conservation and exchange of genetic resources. These policies were strengthened by the 1983 FAO International Undertaking on Plant Genetic Resources viewing plant germplasm as a "heritage of mankind." Subsequently, however, and in the Convention on Biological Diversity of 1992, national sovereignty has been emphasized. Although the Convention excluded materials already in genebanks, obviously the IARCs need to reassess their position as the world's premier holders of food germplasm diversity.

As we noted earlier, the significance of the IARC *ex situ* collections is enormous. The international centres hold about half a million (14%) of the world's 3.8 million stored seed samples, but this amounts to roughly 40% of the unique food-crop germplasm in living collections. Figure 3 describes the global *ex situ* storage situation for plant genetic resources.

If GATT–TRIPS plays out as predicted, many developing countries (the IARCs' priority clients) may adopt some form of IP over plant germplasm. It is feared by some that germplasm provided freely by an IARC could become subject to exclusive monopoly and this, in turn, could constrain free exchange.

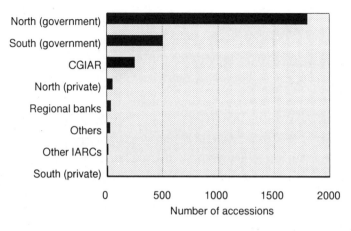

Figure 3. World germplasm holdings by category of holder
(source: Iwanaga 1993).

Furthermore, under GATT–TRIPS, germplasm made available by the IARCs to another public institute or private company could conceivably become incorporated into material protected by the recipient. In this case, the availability of the material to developing countries having IP laws would be constrained. There have been a few instances in which IARC varieties have been protected by private interests without the consent of the IARC. In short, the IARCs may find themselves in circumstances where their gene-bank materials or research could be restricted by others and where profits could accrue inequitably.

The IARCs also confront a second set of concerns. Their genebank accessions are held on behalf of the world community, especially small-scale farmers in developing countries These accessions, however, could conceivably be used as a bargaining

Damned if they do and damned if they don't. IARCs are "a-lateral" institutions caught amidst ambiguous multilateral accords requiring bilateral contracts between nations and corporations.

chip when negotiating technology transfers with private researchers. Some fear that some IARCs will not be able to resist the pressure to use this chip. A side effect of such negotiations could lead to a constraint on genebank access.

Negotiations over transfers of technology pose still other problems. Increasingly, IARCs are discovering that important information related to new agricultural biotechnologies is protected by IP and is often in the hands of private companies. Although some enterprises, such as Monsanto and Merck, have been notably generous in making their research available to developing countries, the raison d'être of companies is not philanthropy, and firms are not eager to surrender high-cost research to IARCs who might cycle back inventions to undercut markets. This is an understandable concern.

Consequently, many public and private institutions want assurances that their IP will be honoured and that the products of their mutual research will also be protected. Some IARCs feel they have no choice but to participate in IP arrangements to ensure that developing countries are not shut off from key new technologies.

A final concern relates to the potential for IARCs to secure additional research funds through IP royalties. In a world of declining agricultural research budgets, IARCs are under pressure to look for new sources of funding. It is tempting for some IARCs to consider recouping some of their R&D costs through Plant Breeders' Rights or patents. Although it is acknowledged that the profits may be limited, there is always the hope that a single invention could make a real difference.

In sum, many IARCs feel they are trapped in a world where IP over biomaterials is becoming the norm, where access to technologies may be conditional on an IARC's ability to negotiate IP arrangements, and where changes in long-standing practices of free germplasm exchange and universal access may undermine the IARC's position in negotiations. The Crucible Group recognizes that these are real and difficult concerns. Some members note that the advent of IP into Third World agriculture is perceived by the IARCs almost entirely as a "problem" rather than an "opportunity," and this may give policymakers some indication of the situation developing countries also face.

Some Crucible members question the capacity of the IARCs to be responsible for the South's biomaterials and to act in the South's best interests. Two factors in particular increase their concern: the Convention on Biological Diversity and the increase in bilateral arrangements, which the Convention has helped to stimulate. The issue of IP has been before the IARCs for more than a decade, but the CGIAR system has not been able to reach a common policy. This is partly because of the distinct and different legal character of each IARC and partly because the overall system has little experience in formulating policy.

The IARCs' discomfort with policy questions could lead to a patchwork, case-by-case approach to IP. Some fear that such approaches could be influenced by perceived or expressed Northern interests, in addition to, or even in conflict with those of developing countries. There is some concern that few national governments, either developed or developing, support PGR programs that could provide reliable alternatives to the IARCs.

There is no distinct scientific or political line separating the improved germplasm provided by farmers and the improved germplasm enhanced by IARC scientists. It would be a violation of responsibility, some believe, if IARCs, after the fact, developed policies allowing some germplasm to become private IP. They argue that IARC trusteeship, under FAO auspices, should mean that only an intergovernmental body can be responsible for the IP policy of those Centres with respect to biomaterials.

Some in the Group express the opinion that, unless a clear policy is established by CGIAR on this issue, IARCs will drift into practices that could prove detrimental to small-scale farmers and developing countries. What is seen as "defensive patenting" one year might become opportunistic patenting a few years later. Critics of the IARCs regard past IARC statements as full of ambiguity. They note that initial statements indicating that IARCs would hold revenues from IP at arms length, or establish an independent fund, have become more vague over time, and have left open the possibility that royalties would flow directly back into IARC programs.

Critics agree however, that it is not the good will but the good judgment of the IARCs that they question. NGO critics, in particular, commended the efforts of the Centre Directors in trying to resolve this policy issue, and note with special appreciation the forthright manner of some IARCs in addressing these problems. In dealing with the IP issue expeditiously, it was suggested that CGIAR could refer to FAO or another appropriate intergovernmental body for resolution.

Other members of the Crucible Group strongly disagree and argue that the IARCs have served the best interests of developing countries for more than two decades and that they have proven their ability to pursue beneficial policies through sound science and to manage political concerns pragmatically and in the best interests of their priority clients. They believe that the nature of the trusteeship in which their collections are held obliges IARCs to act on behalf of farmers and to negotiate access to new technologies for farmers. If IARCs, individually or collectively, conclude that farmers would be hurt by the absence of IP, then the IARCs must develop IP protection.

IARCs must have transparent policies that ensure that any benefit from germplasm exploitation accrues to the countries that donate germplasm.

Defensive Publication

Despite this range of views, several members of the Crucible Group expressed interest in a US alternative known as Statutory Invention Registration or a more formal form of defensive publication. This appears to be a "nonpatent patent" that may meet the needs of some international genebanks. The possibility of such an option was identified by Tim Roberts, a patent expert with extensive commercial experience, and is summarized in Table 2.

Table 2. Defensive Publication.

Patents are granted only for what is new and only to the first inventor. Suppose the inventor is not interested in obtaining a legally enforceable monopoly, but wishes only to make sure that her or his invention cannot be patented by someone else. One option is to publish. In most countries, this makes sure that any patent on the same invention filed after the date of publication will be invalid. In the United States, uniquely, this is not so. A rival inventor may be able to allege prior invention — that is to say, that the invention was made by her or him before the publication date, although no patent application was filed until later.

Another problem that often arises with living material is that of enablement. To invalidate a later patent, a publication must be enabling — it must not merely state that the invention exists but also show how to practice it. A simple description of the properties of a new organism does not enable anyone to reproduce that organism. Nearly always, they will require access to a sample of the organism itself.

For the benefit of inventors who do not want monopoly rights, the US Patent Office has evolved a system of defensive publication termed Statutory Invention Registration (35 USC 157). An applicant for a patent who does not want a monopoly can apply for a patent in the usual way, but also ask for the application to be published without examination for novelty. Before publication, the application is examined to check that the invention is described in a way that enables it to be repeated and that it appears technically useful (not an ornamental design or a perpetual motion machine, for example). After publication, no further action is taken by the US Patent Office, unless another inventor appears with a plausible claim to have made the same invention earlier. In this case, the US Patent Office will declare an "interference," a proceeding to decide which of the two claimants is the first inventor. The advantage of this over publication is that the inventor who publishes establishes invention only as of the date of publication (which may be months or years after the research was done). In an interference, however, both parties can show what they actually did and when.

In this way, the true inventor can protect her or his position in a way in which publication would not have done. The defensive publication forms part of the prior art that the Patent Office is obliged to search. If it is overlooked (which can easily happen, as it is often difficult to tell that two different descriptions refer to the same biological material), the inventor can seek an interference when the rival patent issues. The interference proceeding provides an opportunity to prove, by experimental evidence, that the two inventions are the same. Such evidence would otherwise not be available to the Patent Office.

(continued)

Table 2 concluded

This suggests an opportunity for seedbanks that are concerned about patenting of their material by others. They could file an application in the USA for defensive publication. This would list their accessions and state that samples would be made unrestrictedly available for research purposes to all requesting them. This would confirm the principle of availability of such samples and make it more difficult in practice for third parties to erode this. Note that only one application is necessary, which means that the cost is not prohibitive. The NIH application on 2 000 or so listed DNA sequences has established that there is no objection in principle to a single patent application claiming a large group of disparate biological materials. There is some question as to whether simply saying the samples are available would suffice. Normal rules require the inventor to place samples in a public depository (at a cost of several hundred dollars each) and to promise to replace samples if they die. But the genebanks already function as depositories, so perhaps this is not necessary. Such a defensive filing would not prevent the patenting of genuine inventions based on genebank samples. Inventions based on isolation or discovery of a new gene in such samples or on the use of such materials to produce new varieties with significantly improved properties, could still be patented.

Despite widely differing views on the legal character and capacity of the IARCs, all Crucible Group members were able to agree on some key points.

- The IARCs (and other public genebanks) should explore the possibility of filing a "Defensive Publication" with the US Patent Office, listing all accessions in their genebanks in a single document. Once registered, this patent-like application will make it more difficult for any other party to be granted a patent on any material in the listing: and the IARCs would have formal status to challenge such patents if granted.

- Regardless of the potential for Defensive Publication, the Crucible Group agrees that accessions held in trust in the IARC collections, at least, should not be protectable by IP rights.

- MTAs could play a role in allowing Centres access to new biotechnologies as long as these agreements do not lead to exclusive monopoly protection of materials held in trust through either patents or PBR. The potential for using certain kinds of MTAs to ensure that germplasm remains in the public domain should be further explored.

- The IARCs should urgently continue their efforts to adopt a common and coherent policy with respect to IP, and bring them to a speedy conclusion.

- The CGIAR should encourage and participate fully in the public debate on alternative ways of protecting innovation that avoid high rates of genetic erosion and increase the exchange and use of resources on an equitable basis.

Recommendations

26. The CGIAR is strongly encouraged to quickly conclude clear policies on IP, with respect to germplasm, in accordance with the Convention on Biological Diversity, and taking fully into account the origins of the germplasm for which they have undertaken responsibility.

27. The Crucible Group recommends that IARCs conclude an agreement with the member nations of FAO placing the *ex situ* germplasm collections they hold in trust under the auspices of that intergovernmental body.

28. The Group further recommends that IARCs establish MTA policies in keeping with the Convention on Biological Diversity and, in accordance with their relationship to FAO, that seek to ensure that benefits accrue to the donors of germplasm. IARCs should develop MTAs in consultation with the donors of the germplasm involved and with the intent of ensuring that any financial benefit arising from such MTAs be distributed in keeping with the wishes of the germplasm donor. The objective of MTAs is not to support the programs of the IARCs but to provide new funds and new technologies to developing countries. As far as is possible, MTAs should ensure that beneficial technologies are available to farmers.

DIFFERENT VIEWPOINTS

V. THE GATT–TRIPS COMPLICATION

Will GATT–TRIPS, in imposing IP for plants, harm the South's farmers and agricultural development — or does TRIPS provide benefits and give countries room to set their own course?

Viewpoint A — Removing the Barriers to International Trade

In 1986, the Uruguay Round was launched by more than 100 countries in the belief that a general reduction in national trade barriers would be advantageous to all countries. GATT is a package deal. No country should become a signatory to the trade agreement unless they believe that the overall package is beneficial to their country's development. In the negotiations that began 8 years ago, every country has bargained and traded advantages to achieve the best results.

Traditionally, developing countries have opposed the range of nontariff barriers that have prevented them from exporting commodities and manufactures to industrialized countries. The range of "invisible" barriers have included labeling, licencing and insurance provisions, health regulation, and virtually scores of other intentional or unintentional constraints that have left them on the outside of international trade looking in. Among the most significant barriers to trade and to technology transfer has been the imbalance in the protection of inventions. If innovators cannot receive royalties in a foreign market, they have no reason to transfer their technology to that market and they are effectively barred from trading there. Simultaneously, the foreign market is likely to find itself left to develop with yesterday's technology rather than the more effective and efficient technologies of today. Both parties lose. As TRIPS now stands, signatory states will be expected to adopt an effective IP system for plant varieties, but there are special provisions giving poor countries several extra years to develop appropriate legislation. Countries are not forced to take a protection system that may not suit them: they may choose patents, UPOV-style protection of varieties, or design a special system of their own.

Viewpoint B — Life Patenting is Not a Trade Issue

Trade agreements last a decade, extinction of species is forever. GATT has not undergone some radical reversal. It was unfair in the past and it has only enlarged the scope of its inequity during the Uruguay Round. The South cannot realistically reject a GATT deal unless countries choose to become disadvantaged outsiders to the entire industrialized trading community. Through TRIPS, industrialized countries are usurping the sovereign right of nations to set their own innovation and development policies. Intellectual property for plants means that medicinal plants that protect 80% of poor people and crop plants that feed us all are open to the exclusive monopoly control of companies with the largest legal departments. Formally, such rights are available to all innovators; in reality, they are not open to the poor, because of their poverty. It is uniformly true that foreign multinationals dominate the patent scene in developing countries.

In summary, three tactical initiatives are available to countries if they sign the trade agreement: use the extensive (5 to as much as 20 year) period from now to when GATT is reviewed to strengthen international opposition to the patenting of life forms; explore IP systems that do not permit exclusive monopoly and that compel the national working of inventions where appropriate; and press for countervailing protection for the technical and intellectual contribution and way of life of farmers and indigenous peoples.

Viewpoint C — Grounds for Concern

GATT's intent is that all signatory states adopt an effective IP system for plant varieties. Countries may opt to use existing IP mechanisms for varieties or to define a *sui generis* system. Because other sections of TRIPS refer, by name, to each international IP convention, it is significant that no mention is made of UPOV. Some negotiators believe that UPOV does not adequately protect the interests of breeders, whereas others believe UPOV goes too far. The result is that countries are free to establish their own unique systems recognizing, however, that a review of its effectiveness will be undertaken 4 years after the agreement comes into force. Presumably, ineffective systems could incur trade reprisals.

Because, by and large, the North is not interested in selling seed in the South until a significant market develops, many countries could expect flexible treatment when introducing legislation. Least-developed countries also have a 10-year grace period after

GATT is enacted. Evidently, the formation of a fully staffed and strongly enforced national IP system for plant varieties could be an unacceptable drain on a poor country's human and financial resources — even to the extent of reducing research capacity by pulling scientists away from innovative work to undertake regulatory functions. Sovereign nations must not be pressured into adopting IP for plant varieties. Countries that feel obliged to adopt such laws should make use of the time available to them to determine the IP approach that is to their greatest advantage. This should include a full exploration of *sui generis* options.

VI. WHICH IP IS BEST FOR PLANTS?

If a government determines that some form of IP for plant varieties is either advisable or inevitable to keep in time with GATT, should they opt for patents, or for one of the two UPOV conventions, or for something else altogether?

Viewpoint A — Time May Be on South's Side

Governments feeling GATT pressure to adopt IP should first understand that recent biotechnology claims contain the seeds of self-destruction for biotechnology patents. The several-year period available before legislation is required should be used to publicize the inequities of the systems — not to surrender to them. Although the UPOV Act of 1978 is more flexible than the Act of 1991, governments have only until the end of 1995 to join under the 1978 rules. This "unrepeatable offer" should be avoided, as should UPOV 1991 and industrial patents. The only feasible means of protecting national sovereignty, at this time, is to consider *sui generis* systems that do not require exclusive monopoly while broadening the intergovernmental challenge to IP over life forms.

Viewpoint B — It Depends on the Country

Sovereign countries have the absolute right to adopt or reject IP systems. Should a country deem that it is in its overall best interest to adopt IP, then it should explore all the options available to it without biased prejudgment. It may be, for example, that a country with advanced expertise in plant tissue culture and genetic manipulation would find that a patent mechanism is most appropriate. Another country with an extensive export market for plants, such as cut flowers and other ornamentals, may benefit from the

UPOV Act of 1991. Other countries with less research capacity or a more modest regulatory capability might prefer the UPOV Act of 1978. Some may like to design systems specifically tailored to their own situations. UPOV and WIPO have experts available to work with governments to help them determine the legislation most appropriate to their needs.

Viewpoint C — UPOV 1978 Has Advantages

A country choosing to adopt legislation compatible with the UPOV Act of 1978 will have these advantages: (a) It need not actually join UPOV to be acceptable to GATT. This means that the country need not adopt new laws before the end of 1995 and can take longer to prepare a workable scheme. (b) A country that does join before the closure of the Act of 1978 can always determine, at a later date, to accede to the Act of 1991. The reverse is not the case. (c) UPOV 1978 offers more flexibility in safeguarding the rights of farmers and requires fewer species to be protected. The administrative burden is thus less onerous.

VII. SAVING AND REPLANTING SEEDS

Are seed companies eroding the ancient right of farmers to save harvested seed to trade with neighbours or plant the next season? Or are some unscrupulous farmers–dealers abusing this privilege to camouflage their own seed businesses at the expense of those who did the inventive work?

Viewpoint A — Poor Farmers Do Not Make Breeders Rich

This issue is for countries that adopt IP protection for plant varieties (either patents or Plant Breeders' Rights). Many fear that GATT–TRIPS or other international agreements could exert undue pressure on the South to adopt IP provisions that, in turn, could constrain farmers in the use of protected seed. Everyone agrees that seed saved by Third World farmers, in general, and poor farmers, in particular, for their own use, does not much worry commercial breeders. What companies want to halt is the unauthorized sale of protected seed for replanting. They say that allowing the replanting of successive generations of seed undercuts markets for new varieties. They contend that, in this era of high-performance, biotechnology-based seeds, it is not in the long-term interests of anyone (farmers, consumers, or governments) to discourage innovation in this way. In their view, private research investment requires the possibility of reliable, repeat sales of good varieties. This is a Northern perspective, but, improperly interpreted, it could impinge on the South and impair, directly or indirectly, the capacity and choices of farmers as creators and conservers of diversity. Given a universal desire to ensure that poor farmers of the Third World retain their traditional freedoms, it should be possible to use international conventions and national legislation flexibly to allow such farmers to retain their seed for subsequent seasons and to exchange seed, as they wish, within their own district.

Viewpoint B — The Reasonable Right of Breeders to Their Inventions

This is an ofter misunderstood and distorted issue in plant breeding. Any country that chooses to adopt IP protection for plant varieties does so because it believes that this will encourage breeders to develop nationally beneficial new varieties by offering inventors a fair opportunity to recoup their investment. In response to such legislation in the North, breeders have stepped up their research commitment and employed expensive new biotechnologies in the service of improved yields, increased hardiness, and food quality. In industrialized countries that have had IP protection for plant varieties for several decades, both farmers and governments seem happy with the experience.

The South, by and large, is not an area of direct interest to international breeders until a sizeable commercial seed market develops. Many modern varieties, however, could be developed with specific adaptation to national conditions through collaborative research between international firms and national governments or local seed enterprises. In such cases, the national enterprise — far more than its international partner — will not want to have its small market opportunity undercut by competitors operating under the facade of the farmer's right to save seed. No one wants to deny poor farmers the opportunity to retain seed from one harvest for the next planting season — or to use protected varieties as a source of variation to develop their own locally adapted varieties. In fact, this should be encouraged. Governments and local companies can work together to ensure that this important, traditional practice continues and is strengthened.

oint C — The Vanishing Rights of Farmers

eat to farmers means that the risk of introducing IP monop-
unacceptable. In the 1970s, the seed industry acknowledged
ners' right to save and sell company-bred seed. In the 1980s,
ners' "right" became a "privilege" as companies failed to
ze cereals. Corporations complained that, because seeds are
al "photo-copiers," farmers could hijack the resale market
r varieties. Today, the revised UPOV convention argues that
d be illegal for farmers to save seed of protected varieties
POV 1991b). TRIPS requires (in certain circumstances) that
den of proof should be laid, not on the accusing company,
he accused farmer. In spite of Agenda 21, the prospect is for
age of oppression in which farmers become renters of
sm contracting to the subsidiaries of international compa-
seed and chemicals and returning their harvest to the trade
cessing subsidiaries of the same multinational.

inationals are primarily targeting seed markets in indus-
rial d countries. GATT–TRIPS and the Convention on Biological
Diversity, however, could impose the same pressures on the South.
Third World countries, now being pressed to adopt UPOV 1991,
will not have the resources necessary to prevent corporate abuse.
The system pits small farming communities against both multinationals and national licensees. Farmers have the absolute right to
save seed, to experiment with exotic germplasm, and to exchange
seed with neighbouring communities. To deny these rights is to cut
the heart out of global conservation and enhancement of plant
biodiversity.

VIII. IP RIGHTS AND OBLIGATIONS

Do both society and inventors have a fair deal? Is the balance of
rights and obligations as it should be, or do changes have to be
made?

Viewpoint A — Matching Rights with Obligations

The history of IP systems has been one of continual strengthening
of corporate monopolies and the weakening of the rights of society.
This is particularly the case with biological diversity. Once completely out of the realm of IP protection and considered as common
heritage to be shared freely for the benefit of all, now that same
diversity is under threat of being monopolized by a limited num-

ber of corporations that have the means to make most profit on it. Society as a whole but especially the rural poor that have developed and maintained biodiversity for millennia are the ones that risk to lose most in the continuous strengthening of current IP systems. With respect to biodiversity, it is an urgent necessity to complement any rights that companies derive from IP with a series of obligations to participate fully in the task of saving the world's biological diversity. This could be done through a legally binding Code of Conduct on Germplasm Introductions, to be developed by FAO or the partners in the Convention on Biological Diversity and to become part of IP conventions and national legislation.

Such a code should include requirements that breeders (public, private, national, or foreign) introducing new varieties produce an Environmental Impact Report with an assessment of the planned introduction on genetic erosion of locally used varieties. If it is determined that the newly introduced variety will displace farmers' varieties or other forms of biodiversity that have not been adequately collected or studied, the breeder of the introduced variety should be expected to contribute to the conservation effort. Genetic uniformity ceilings should also be established. Whenever the genetic uniformity of a crop in an ecological zone becomes too great, governments should prohibit the marketing of the least beneficial varieties and take whatever measures they deem necessary to encourage breeding diversity. To facilitate this task, breeders should provide a complete genetic disclosure; that is, a detailed pedigree of every new variety to be introduced. National patent offices in major industrialized countries, as well as the international IP conventions, should incorporate a public defender to represent the interests of farmers, indigenous peoples, and the South, in general, with respect to biological product and processes.

Viewpoint B — Maintaining the Balance

The balance of benefits between inventors and society must be, and be seen to be, fair. There is a growing perception of imbalance that, justified or not, could prove damaging to the long-term interests of inventors. It is important for all parties to make their concerns clear and for society's confidence in inventor incentives to be restored. The recent trends to extend IP protection to biological diversity create a new situation in the rights–obligation balance as it is clearly more difficult to establish clear criteria for living resources than it is for inanimate objects.

In general, the real implications of extending IP protection to life forms are poorly understood. Overall, IP systems offer an efficient and fair approach to reward those putting substantial effort into developing biodiversity. Adjustments to the current systems, however, might be needed, especially to ensure that "informal innovators" at the community level receive a fair treatment for their innovative activities in developing and maintaining biodiversity. We need in-depth studies and proposals on how this can be done. Possibilities include opening up the current IP systems for informal innovation or creating separate but parallel mechanisms to support it.

Viewpoint C — Society's Obligations

Under existing IP systems, inventors already have a whole series of obligations to cope with. Depending on the specific IP right, they include the obligation to disclose, fully, the steps of the invention so that another person with reasonable competence in the field can replicate the invention; the obligation, in the case of biological inventions, to deposit a sample of the invention in an authorized public repository; the obligation to ensure that inventions are "worked" or to forfeit control of the invention; the obligation to bear the whole cost of establishing, maintaining, and defending the right without burden on the public purse; the obligation to allow other researchers, including competitors, access to the invention for research purposes; and the obligation to surrender, forever, control over the commercialization of a plant invention after a period ranging from one to three decades depending on the country. No one is suggesting that these obligations should be weakened. Indeed, parts of industry complain because they are not always properly enforced.

Over the course of the last few decades, the costs of research have doubled and tripled, the regulatory burden and time delays in obtaining protection and receiving permission to commercialize have lengthened, and the effectiveness of IP systems has deteriorated. Any discussion of obligations must include the obligations of society to act reasonably with respect to the rights of inventors. Intellectual property systems offer society a completely inventor-financed incentive system. The task of innovators today is hard enough as it is — society will lose, not gain, by imposing additional burdens on them.

IX. THE MERCK–INBIO AGREEMENT

Is the Merck–InBio Bioprospecting Contract just a more sophisticated form of biopiracy or does it represent a realistic best-effort
for a functional relationship between companies and countries?

In a much discussed 2-year agreement announced in 1991,
Merck, the largest pharmaceutical company in the world, paid
$1.135 million for biodiversity exploration to InBio, a nonprofit
NGO in Costa Rica (Reid 1993). In turn, InBio will provide Merck
with 10 000 biosamples from Costa Rica's nature parks, which
Merck will scan for any commercially interesting drug compo-
nents. If any profitable drug is developed from this material, the
company will have the sole right to market it, although an undis-
closed percentage of the royalties will be shared with InBio.

Viewpoint A — A Rip-Off!

This deal is no more than a rip-off of the South's biological treasure
and the local people that depend on it. Merck's sales in 1991 were
$8.6 billion, whereas Costa Rica's gross national product (GNP)
that year was $5.2 billion (Mussey 1992). Merck's research budget
in 1991 was roughly $1 billion. Pharmaceutical companies invest
an average of $231 million on research for each new drug. Although
nearly all of this goes on proving safety and efficacy, rather than on
the initial discovery, nevertheless, the discovery charge for one
single new drug arising from the deal is barely loose change
(DeMassi et al. 1991). Noncommercial plant-collection costs often
run to $400 per sample for crop species. For Merck, who gets the
samples for $113 each, the Costa Rica contract is cheap labour, even
if it is more than is usually paid. If, 20 years from now, there is a
dispute over the origin of a plant-derived active ingredient (Nica-
ragua, Honduras, or Costa Rica?) the country's capacity to appeal
to the courts is poor. Merck may well have more patent lawyers
than can be found in all of Costa Rica.

This and many similar deals that are now being struck to cash
in on the world's biodiversity undermine many of the agreements
reached at Rio. Although Agenda 21 and the Convention on Biological Diversity are efforts to agree collectively and multilaterally
on how to save the environment, and what to pay for it, the
bilateralism embodied in these contracts effectively constitute a
"divide and conquer" strategy to get the goods cheap. Although
the UNCED results are full of promises and commitments to
recognize, support, and compensate indigenous people for their

role in saving and using biodiversity, hardly any of these bilateral deals even mention them. The deals are mostly done between companies in the North and formal research or conservation institutes in the South, and any cash resulting from them tends to reinforce traditional conservation schemes that throw indigenous people out of biodiversity areas, rather than supporting them or working in alliance with them.

Viewpoint B — Finally We Start Doing Something

More than a decade of intergovernmental efforts to establish an equitable system for biodiversity conservation has produced nothing tangible. In this one initiative, a major company working with a national NGO and a concerned government has yielded more direct financial support for conservation and development than all of the talk and funding for Farmers' Rights. The net effect, so far, is that a number of Costa Ricans are receiving useful training in parataxonomy, scientists are being trained, laboratory equipment is being purchased, and significant new money is going into national biodiversity conservation priorities. Costa Rica's royalty share from any commercial drugs resulting from the deal, has not been disclosed, but some observers suggest that the country could, if 10 successful drugs are developed, earn more per year from royalties than from their coffee or banana exports (Axt et al. 1993).

Others are learning from the initiative and are negotiating their own contracts. At long last, there is money on the table and work is being done. Biodiversity requires a diversity of initiatives and the world community should welcome and encourage all of them. None of these initiatives precludes multilateral programs (intrinsically more difficult to set up), and all are being developed with full adherence to and respect for the United Nations' Convention on Biological Diversity. Those who oppose this kind of deal are afraid of political diversity and are trapped in the straightjacket of their own "political correctness" to the detriment of biological diversity and national development.

Viewpoint C — Keep All Options Open

The Merck–Costa Rica agreement has galvanized a healthy debate while moving the world from theory to practice. Whether the agreement will withstand the test of time or not is unknown. It is encouraging that about one-third of the money will go for equipment and almost one-quarter will go to salaries and training for local people as well as scientists. Another quarter is available directly for conservation and for infrastructure support.

Nevertheless, the deal has inadvertently contributed to an environment of "bilateralism" that could pit one country against another. There is a false sense of "impending profit" from bilateral deals that could distort intergovernmental negotiations. If so, many countries in the South may find themselves without corporate partners and without access to multilateral funds to safeguard the biodiversity essential to their own well-being. Only a handful of countries and companies are likely to benefit from bilateral contracts. The net effect could be a short-term approach to selective biodiversity conservation and the long-term loss of global biological diversity resources. Without denigrating or discouraging new initiatives, the world community must act to ensure that Agenda 21, the Convention on Biological Diversity, and the revised Global Environmental Facility remain true to their global responsibilities and that intergovernmental negotiations take into account, and build upon, our collective experiences.

X. INTERNATIONAL GERMPLASM COLLECTIONS

The IARCs of the CGIAR are working with FAO to affirm their trusteeship of genebank accessions. Will this move help assure the continued global availability of germplasm collections? What are the consequences for CGIAR policies on IP protection?

Viewpoint A — Strengthening International Trusteeship

The CGIAR Centres hold, in trust on behalf of the international community, the world's largest international collection of crop and forest germplasm — more than 500 000 accessions. About 600 000 accessions and breeding lines are made available free of charge to researchers every year, mostly in developing countries (1993 IPGRI data). Since their inception, the Centres have worked with governments and scientists to collect, conserve, and enhance germplasm for the benefit of developing-country farmers. Governed by trustees from more than 60 countries, about half from the South, and with funding from about 40 countries (including eight developing countries), intergovernmental institutions, and private foundations, the CGIAR is the largest conservation and breeding body working on behalf of the South. The CGIAR has trained more than 50 000 agricultural researchers and has worked with national agricultural research services to feed at least 500 million people in the

South who would not otherwise be fed (Anderson et al. 1988).

The CGIAR system is aware that the global research environment is changing and that the advent of new biotechnologies has meant a shift toward private-sector research. Private investors have an understandable interest in IP, and this has raised special concerns for publicly financed international institutes such as the CGIAR. To ensure that the integrity of Centre genebanks is not impugned by future collaborative research initiatives, the Centres have approached FAO and proposed that the genebank accessions be placed under the auspices of that intergovernmental body, which, under conditions of trusteeship, would return responsibility for them to the Centres. The move is intended to guarantee that genebank samples cannot be subjected to exclusive monopoly under an IP system. There can be no reasonable objections, however, to private companies receiving germplasm from genebanks, using it in further innovative breeding, and seeking IP protection for the result.

Viewpoint B — An Unreliable Partner and a Dangerous Trend

The CGIAR system has no collective legal identity. Sixteen of its eighteen Centre Chairs and 14 of 18 Centre Directors-General are from the North; more than one-quarter of all Centre Trustees come from four like-minded countries — Australia, Canada, the UK, and the USA. Almost two-thirds of the Centre Chairs and Directors also come from these four countries (CGIAR 1993). After more than two decades of work headquartered in the South, most IARCs function more like mid-western US or Australian universities than truly international institutes. It is simply unacceptable for the North's donors to pretend they know what is best for the South's farmers. The CGIAR system must come under intergovernmental policy oversight.

The FAO–CGIAR initiative to place IARC genebanks under FAO auspices is to be applauded. Trusteeship, however, should be reviewable and based upon performance. The result should not be that genebank collections are left open for the use of everyone — including private companies — while the products of IARC research are subjected to IP monopolies. Before trusteeship is recognized by FAO, the CGIAR system should acknowledge that there exists no clear scientific distinction between germplasm in a genebank and that same material removed to a breeding program — or germplasm later developed into new commercial varieties. It is one continuum, and it is unfair if the front end is "free" and the end-product is patented by any party, private or public. The CGIAR system should reject IP and establish policies that ensure that their research is not high-jacked by private interests in the North.

Viewpoint C — A Reasonable Process

The CGIAR–FAO decision to place genebank collections, held in trust by the Centres, under the auspices of FAO is a reasonable and even far-sighted policy initiative. The effect will be to ensure that the unilateral actions of a host government cannot threaten global access to genebanks. Also, base collections will be permanently kept in the public domain and will not be subjected to IP claims. Through FAO, the international community will have the right to review arrangements related to genebank safety and access and to be consulted on relevant policy issues.

There is legitimate ground to question whether a trusteeship agreement that only removes bank accessions from IP claim could be interpreted as acquiescence of an IARC policy to enter into IP agreements related to improved germplasm. Whether this is an appropriate policy or not is a separate issue. There is also cause to question whether or not an agreement between FAO and 18 separate Centres might give the inaccurate impression that each Centre has the same policy on IP. This is not now true. The CGIAR system has been struggling to formulate a common policy for several years. To ensure the trust of the international community, CGIAR must put a common policy in place as quickly as possible. It should also look closely at MTAs to be certain that the downstream interests arising from genebank collections and collaboration with the South are protected in contractual arrangements with parties in the North.

Appendices

1.

A Brief Chronology of the Patent Debate in the North

7th century BC	Greeks permit a 1-year monopoly over cooking recipes
1474	First Patent Law established (Venice)
1623	Statute of Monopolies creates patent provisions for England
1790	First US Patent Act passed in compliance with American Constitution
1790–1850	Industrial patent laws established in many European states
1850–1873	Patent laws revoked or monopoly restricted in several European states
1873	Patent Congress at the Vienna World's Fair adopts compulsory licence compromise to overcome opposition to the industrial patent system
1883	A global patent system is established in the Paris Union
1900	Paris Union is amended and strengthened at Brussels meeting
1911	Paris Union is strengthened again at Washington meeting

1922	Germany accepts a process patent on a bacterium and a meeting of patent lawyers in London moots the possibility of protection for plant varieties
1925	Paris Union is amended and strengthened again in The Hague
1930	United States adopts the Plant Patent Act for fruits and ornamentals
1934	Paris Union is strengthened at its London meeting and definition of patentable material is extended to include flowers and flour
1961	Union for the Protection of New Varieties of Plants (UPOV) is established at Paris meeting
1969	Germany accepts process patents for the breeding of animals
1970	Patent Cooperation Treaty approved by 35 countries at Washington meeting
1972	UPOV Convention is modified and strengthened
1978	UPOV Convention strengthened again
1980	US Supreme Court accepts the patenting of microorganisms
1987	US Patent Office expresses willingness to consider patents on animals
1991	UPOV Convention strengthened to, among other things, stop farmers from replanting protected varieties
1992	"Species" patent granted in the United States on genetically modified cotton
1993	US Government applies for patent rights over human cell lines of citizens of Panama, Papua New Guinea, and the Solomon Islands
1993	GATT agreement includes stipulation that all signatory states must have an IP system for plant varieties and for microorganisms
1994	Second "species" patent granted in Europe on the soybean crop — the first time a species patent is granted on a food crop

2.

THE BIODIVERSITY CONVENTION

Aim (Article 1)

- Conservation of biological diversity

- Sustainable use of variability within and among species and ecosystems

- Fair and equitable sharing of benefits arising out of the utilization of genetic resources, including appropriate access to genetic resources and transfer of relevant technologies and appropriate funding

Partnership

Between the developed country parties that have biotechnology (Article 16) and finance (Article 20) and the developing country parties that have biodiversity (Articles 3 and 15)

Obligations

- The development of national strategies, plans or programs for the conservation and sustainable use of biodiversity (Article 6)

- The identification and monitoring of biodiversity (Article 7)

- In situ conservation (of biodiversity) (Article 8) and *ex situ* conservation (Article 9)

- Research and training (Article 12) and public education (Article 13)

- Assessment of impact on biodiversity of development projects (Article 14)

- Respect of IP rights, wherever they are nationally recognized, which must, however, conform to the objectives of the Convention (Article 16)

- Information exchange (Article 17)

- Technical and scientific cooperation (Article 18)

3.
TRIPS — TRADE-RELATED IP

The objective of TRIPS is to provide minimum standards for member countries in most forms of IP. Here we consider mainly patents and Plant Variety Protection (PVP).

TRIPS lays down basic principles, specific rules for various rights, and rules on enforcement of rights, on maintaining rights, and on transitional arrangements.

Principles

All member countries must treat nationals of other member countries as they treat their own, without any discrimination. Intellectual property should contribute to innovation; to transfer of technology, to social and economic welfare and to a balance of rights and obligations.

Patents

What must be protected?

- Inventions in *all* fields of technology, except:
    - methods for curing humans and animals
    - plants and animals, and essentially biological processes for producing them
- Microorganisms and microbiological processes must be protected
- Plant varieties must also be protected, either by patents or by "an effective *sui generis* system."

The term "an effective *sui generis* system" is not very clear. No doubt it includes UPOV-style protection, but it may also allow more innovative alternatives. What "effective" means will probably in the end be judged by the council of TRIPS.

Countries may also exclude patents on inventions whose exploitation it is necessary to prevent: provided such exploitation would injure public order or morality; or human, animal, or plant life; or seriously damage the environment. However, excluding inventions from patenting because rights over them are considered immoral is not provided for.

Patent Rights

Minimum rights for patentees are laid down. Exceptions must be limited, and not unreasonably conflict with normal exploitation or prejudice the patentee's interests. Compulsory licencing is regulated in detail. The minimum term of patent protection is to be 20 years from filing. For process patents, the burden of proof must be shifted to accused infringers in at least one of two cases:

- If the product of the process is new or

- If the owner of the patent cannot show what process was actually used, but it is likely that the patented process was used.

Patent Enforcement

Detailed provisions are intended to make it easier to enforce IP rights. Remedies must include damages and injunctions against further infringement, including interim injunctions to preserve the patentee's rights until trial. However, criminal penalties are only required for serious trademark or copyright counterfeiting.

Transitional Arrangements

Equal treatment comes into effect everywhere on signing. Other provisions must be introduced within 1 year, except for developing countries (5 years). Developing countries may also delay the extension of patent rights to new areas of technology for a further 5 years. Least-developed countries need not change their laws for 10 years and may seek further extensions, if required.

Independently of the foregoing, the patentability of plants and animals is to be reviewed 4 years after the agreement comes into force.

Parties are required to provide incentives for transfer of technology to least-developed countries and to provide (when requested and on agreed terms) technical and financial cooperation to developing countries on IP matters.

4.

NATIONAL–INTERNATIONAL SEED ENTERPRISES: PERSPECTIVE FROM THE PRIVATE SECTOR

To encourage development of the private seed industry, governments should first survey the state of agriculture, by crop and by socioeconomic region, to determine which crops and parts of their country can benefit from a private seed industry. For any crop, the existence of dependable markets, relatively large areas of cultivation, and desire on the farmers' part to increase yields through cultural and varietal changes could be signs that farmers might benefit from the presence of private seed firms. Additionally, profit to farmers should be great enough that they can afford to pay a higher price for seed. In brief, commercial seeds are best suited to profitable crops in favourable farming regions.

To attract seed firms, governments should be politically stable and the nation's infrastructure, particularly transportation, should be adequate for the delivery of goods and services to the farming community. There should also be evidence that markets for the crop are relatively stable, without undue interference from either government regulations or private-market manipulators. The presence of public plant-breeding research will be an asset to private seed firms. Farmers will have become accustomed to the introduction of improved varieties and to learning new ways of growing them. Small-scale seed firms, in particular, will depend on public plant-research institutions for advanced breeding materials or even new varieties, as well as for knowledge of new, improved agronomic techniques applied to the new varieties. All seed firms will benefit from germplasm enhancement efforts of the public plant-research institutions. In brief, a strong public plant-breeding research program is necessary for long-range success of the private seed industry.

National encouragement of a full line of improved agricultural practices (for seed cleaning, times and rates of sowing, harvest and storage of product, and efficient marketing) will set the stage for entrepreneurial, small-scale seed companies to add their product to the mix of increasingly sophisticated practices in the commercial farming community. (The understanding here is that shifting to commercial agriculture requires new kinds of sophistication.)

IP laws are not a first requirement for attracting the seed industry to a nation. Seed firms usually start out by dealing in hybrid crops, with built-in property protection, because the seeds must be bought fresh each season, and the parents can be kept as private property. They then may move into selling seeds of self- or open-pollinating crops that perform best when the seed comes from skilled seed producers able to provide weed-free seed with good germination, trueness to type, and a guarantee that the seed is the variety stated. Following this step, farmers and seed companies may be able to benefit from the introduction of fairly written and well-administered IP laws applied to plants. To attract development of local and international seed companies, governments could set up a national consultative group on agricultural research composed of representatives of farmers and both public and private institutions.

5.

COMPARISON OF MAIN PROVISIONS OF PBR UNDER UPOV 1978 AND 1991, AND PATENT LAW

Provisions	UPOV 1978	UPOV 1991	Patent law
Protection coverage	Plant varieties of nationally defined species	Plant varieties of all genera and species	Inventions
Requirements	Distinctness Uniformity Stability	Novelty Distinctness Uniformity Stability	Novelty Inventiveness Nonobviousness
Protection term	Min. 15 years	Min. 20 years	17–20 years (OECD)
Protection scope	Commercial use of *reproductive material* of the variety	Commercial use of *all material* of the variety	Commercial use of protected matter
Breeders' exemption	Yes	Not for *essentially derived* varieties	No
Farmers' "privilege"	Yes	No. Up to national laws	No
Prohibition of double protection	Any species eligible for PBR protection cannot be patented	—	—

Source: Derived from van Wijk and Junne (1992, p. 81).

6.
PATENTS ON PLANTS

Description

Intellectual Property rights are justified, in part, as a human right and, in part, as a contract or bargain with the public. The originator gives to the public something new that it would not otherwise have had. In return, the public gives to the originator limited rights in the "new thing" for a limited period (such as 20 years). The originator is rewarded by exploiting these rights in person, or allowing others to exploit them, for a fee.

If the public is not interested in buying the new article, or if its price is set too high, the inventor receives no reward. The reward is self-regulating — it is determined by public demand for the new product. No one has to judge what the invention is worth — the market does this.

For the system to work, however, several assumptions must be made. These include

- A market economy,

- Appropriate scope and term of rights awarded, and

- Careful fulfilment of the conditions imposed on grant.

In the 1980s, developed countries began to grant patents on life forms and on constituents of life forms (such as DNA sequences, cells, and so forth). It is now proposed to extend this practice to all the members of GATT. The issue is to what extent, if at all, this is justified. What is currently happening, and how does it relate to classical patent law?

To get a patent of any kind, one must make an invention that is new, inventive (not obvious or routine), and be willing and able to describe to others how to make use of it. A patent must not stop people doing what they were doing before — this is fundamental to the bargain with the public. Patents are granted for inventions but not for discoveries. There is a clear distinction:

- A discovery is new knowledge.

- An invention is a new process or product.

Frequently, however, new knowledge will suggest a new thing. Thus many inventions are based on discoveries. The discovery that substance X cures ulcers suggests the invention of a stomach pill containing substance X. This invention is based on a discovery, but that will not mean that it may not be patented. Provided the discovery is new and unexpected, that will allow patenting the invention to which it gives rise.

This distinction is important to keep in mind when considering how genes may be patented. The sequence of a gene is a discovery, pure and simple. It is knowledge about something that already exists. However, it may enable new things to be produced, and these may in principle be patented.

There follows a list of what is currently being patented in Europe and the United States, and what might be patented under TRIPS. Only broad guidance can be given, and little is settled beyond all doubt.

Genes

Natural genes cannot be patented as such. They already exist, they are not new, they are discovered, not invented. (This does not apply to engineered genes. So far, these are much less common, and usually consist of two or three segments of natural genes linked together.) What then is "a patent on a gene"? Generally, what is claimed is not the gene as such but the gene isolated from its natural surroundings and products containing this isolated gene. (The claims are not always worded like that.) Gene inventions of this sort are patented in both Europe and the United States, and will be patented under TRIPS.

Plant Cells

New plant cells — containing transformed DNA, say, or being the product of cell fusion, or in the form of a cell culture — are patented in both Europe and the United States, and could be allowed under TRIPS.

Plants are considered patentable in the United States, and in Europe, although this is contentious. The European Patent Convention (EPC) (Section 53) excludes patents on plant varieties, but the European Patent Office interprets this narrowly. Patents are granted on plants, provided they do not meet the strict UPOV criteria for plant varieties (see below). TRIPS does not require patents on plants, provided plant varieties can be protected by "a *sui generis* system," for example, UPOV.

The EPC further provides that "essentially biological processes" and their products are not patentable. "Microbiological processes" (and their products), however, are patentable. The result of this is that plants obtained by conventional breeding are not patented, but plants modified by gene technology are. Either gene technology is not "essentially biological" — judged by the degree of human intervention in the process — or it is "microbiological" or maybe both. In the United States, there is no bar on patenting plants in any form, or breeding processes. In consequence, patents are granted on plant varieties produced by conventional breeding. A case could be made that such inventions are mostly obvious, but often such patents are accepted with little or no argument.

Increasingly, patents on such plants with new traits are granted in the United States. Similar patents may be granted in Europe, if the plants are the product of gene technology. This is a matter of considerable controversy, particularly where the new trait is obviously desirable and is also the only new feature. It is not usual to grant patents on machines or chemicals defined solely by novel properties (such as anticancer activity or fuel economy). Instead, the patent claims define the chemical structure that results in the improvement. Many believe that plants should be treated in the same way.

7.
TRADE SECRETS AND MATERIAL
TRANSFER AGREEMENTS

Most IP is protected by a formal system, based on specially enacted laws. Where such laws do not exist, it is still possible for an innovator to retain some protection against competitors — provided he can keep his invention secret. If he knows the best way of doing something, he is not generally obliged to tell others about it. A secret manufacturing process or formulation or recipe can give a commercial advantage, as long as others do not know of it.

An advantage of trade secrets to the innovator is that they can last a long time. The corresponding disadvantage is that they are increasingly difficult to keep — they may become public either by analysis of the product sold, disclosure by employees, or even by independent invention by someone else. The disadvantage is that the public loses the opportunity to use the innovator's knowledge in other ways. Licencing of trade secrets is possible, indeed common, though it risks the secret becoming known.

Despite its disadvantages, trade secrecy is still widely used, even where alternatives are available. It is particularly important in the case of biological materials that are not sold, but only used in production. For example, a particular strain of microorganism used to make a drug, or a parent maize line used to make a hybrid, can usually be kept as the secret property of the originator. In such cases, the inventor may prefer trade secrecy to patenting, as patenting requires the invention to be published.

How is trade secrecy maintained? In the first place, the innovator binds staff by contract not to disclose secrets, or use them independently, or pass them on to subsequent employers. However, the innovator cannot require staff to treat as secret what is not so in fact. If the secret becomes known, all can then use it.

Where the trade secret takes the form of a proprietary material (such as a microorganism, gene construct, or seed) it will be transferred (if at all) under a confidentiality or materials transfer agreement. Anglo-Saxon law, broadly, assumes that parties may make any agreement that suits them. If one party wants something badly enough, the other party may name a price. Hence, a party seeking access to the material may be asked to undertake various obligations. These may include not transferring the material.

GLOSSARY

Agenda 21: A comprehensive set of programs of action to promote sustainable development into the 21st ccentury. Although non-binding, Agenda 21 is an important document representing a consensus of the world's governments.

biodiversity: All species of plants and animals, their genetic material, and the ecosystems of which they are a part.

Convention on Biological Diversity: Adopted in Nairobi on 22 May 1992, the Convention was opened for signature and signed during the Rio Earth Summit by over 150 countries. The Convention is a legally binding agreement for conservation and sustainable use of biodiversity. It came into force on 29 December 1993.

DNA (deoxyribonucleic acid): The molecule in chromosomes that is the repository of genetic information in all organisms (with the exception of a small number of viruses, in which the hereditary material is ribonucleic acid, RNA). The information coded by DNA determines the structure and function of an organism.

***ex situ* ("off-site")**: This refers, for example, to conservation of genetic resources outside of their natural habitats. Gene banks and botanical gardens hold *ex situ* collections.

gene: The fundamental physical and functional unit of hereditary; the portion of a DNA molecule that is made up of an ordered sequence of nucleotide based pairs that produce a specific product or have an assigned function.

genebank: For plants and seeds, usually a temperature- and humidity-controlled facility used to store seed (or other reproductive materials) for future use in research and breeding programmes. Also called a seedbank.

germplasm: The total genetic variability, represented by germ cells or seeds, available to a particular population of organisms.

Guaymi General Congress: Represents Panama's largest indigenous peoples' organization.

hybrid: Any intermediate plant resulting from crossing two or more different biotypes of the same species or biotypes from two different species.

in situ **("on-site")**: *In situ* conservation means the conservation of ecosystems and natural habitats and the maintenance and recovery of viable populations of species in their natural surroundings and, in the case of domesticated or cultivated species, in the surroundings where they have developed their distinctive properties.

in vitro: By derivation, means "in glass." In general, applied to biological processes when they are experimentally made to occur in isolation from the whole organism (which usually means within a glass vessel). For example, the activities of cells in tissue culture occur *in vitro*.

Rio Earth Summit: The United Nations Conference on Environment and Development (UNCED) and parallel NGO meetings, held in Rio de Janeiro, Brazil in June 1992.

sui generis **legislation**: A unique form of intellectual property protection, especially designed to meet certain criteria and needs.

ACRONYMS

ACIAR	Australian Centre for International Agricultural Research
CGIAR	Consultative Group on International Agricultural Research
CIPR	Community Intellectual Property Rights
COMMUTECH	Community Technology Development Association
DGIS	Directorate General for International Cooperation
DNA	deoxyribonucleic acid
EPC	European Patent Convention
FAO	Food and Agriculture Organization of the United Nations
GATT	General Agreement on Tariffs and Trade
GIFTS	Germplasm, Information, Funds, Technologies, and Systems
GNP	gross national product
GRAIN	Genetic Resources Action International
IARCs	international agricultural research centres
IBPGR	International Board for Plant Genetic Resources
ICI	Imperial Chemical Industries
IDRC	International Development Research Centre
IP	intellectual property

IPGRI	International Plant Genetics Resources Institute
IUPGR	International Undertaking on Plant Genetic Resources
MTA	Material Transfer Agreement
NGO	nongovernmental organization
NIH	National Institutes of Health (United States)
OECD	Organisation for Economic Co-operation and Development
PBR	Plant Breeders' Rights
PGR	plant genetic resources
PVP	Plant Variety Protection
R&D	research and development
RAFI	Rural Advancement Foundation International
SAREC	Swedish Agency for Research Cooperation with Developing Countries
SDC	Swiss Development Corporation
TRIPS	Trade-Related Intellectual Property
UNCED	United Nations Conference on Environment and Development (also known as the Earth Summit)
Unesco	United Nations Educational, Scientific and Cultural Organisation
UPOV	Union for the Protection of New Varieties of Plants
USAID	United States Agency for International Development
WIPO	World Intellectual Property Organization

BIBLIOGRAPHY

AAS (African Academy of Sciences). 1989. Farmers also experiment: a neglected intellectual resource in African science. Academy Science Publishers, Nairobi, Kenya. Discovery and Innovation, 1(1), 19–25.

Anderson, J.R.; Herdt, R.W.; Scobie, G.M. 1988. Science and food — the CGIAR and its partners. World Bank, Washington, DC, USA.

Axt, J.R.; Corn, M.L.; Lee, M.; Ackerman, D.M. 1993. Biotechnology, indigenous peoples and intellectual property rights. Congressional Research Service, Washington, DC, USA. Report for Congress, 16 April 1993.

Berg, T.; Bjornstad, A.; Fowler, C.; Skroppa, T. 1991. Technology options and the gene struggle. NorAgric, Norwegian Centre for International Agricultural Development, Agricultural University of Norway, Aas, Norway. Development and Environment No. 8.

CGIAR (Consultative Group on International Agricultural Research). 1993. The Boards of Trustees of the international agricultural research centres. CGIAR Secretariat, Washington, DC, USA.

Cunningham, A.B. 1993. Ethics, ethnobiological research, and biodiversity. Worldwide Fund for Nature, Washington, DC, USA.

Daes, E.-I.A. 1993. Study of the protection of the cultural and intellectual property of indigenous peoples. UN Commission on Human Rights, New York, NY, USA. E/CN. 4/Sub.2/1993/28.

Davies, A.G.; Richards, P. 1991. Rain forest in Mende life: resources and subsistence strategies in rural communities around the Gola North Forest Reserve (Sierra Leone). A report to the Economic and Social Committee on Overseas Research (ESCOR). Overseas Development Administration, London, UK.

Davis, S.D.; Droop, S.J.M.; Gregerson, P.; Henson, L; Leon, C.J.; Villa-Lobos, J.L.; Synge, H.; Zantovaska, J. 1986. Plants in danger: what do we know? World Conservation Union, Gland, Switzerland.

DeMassi, J.; Hansan, R.W.; Grabowski, H.G.; Lassagna, L. 1991. Costs of innovation in the pharmaceutical industry. Journal of Health Economics, 10, 107.

Deusing, J. 1992. Agro food industry hi-tech. Ciba-Geigy, Basel, Switzerland.

FAO (Food and Agriculture Organization of the United Nations). 1991. AGROSTAT Database on Food Balance Sheets (Intake). FAO, Rome, Italy.

Fox, J. 1994. NIH nixes human DNA patents: what next? Bio/Technology, 12 (April), 348.

Gadbow, R.M.; Richards, T.J., ed. 1990. Intellectual property rights — global consensus, global conflict? Westview Press, Boulder, CO, USA.

Industrial Bioprocessing. 1993. USDA researcher seeks rubber-growing CRADA partners. Industrial Bioprocessing, 1993 (January), 6.

IPGRI (International Plant Genetic Resources Institute). 1993. Diversity for development: the strategy of the International Plant Genetic Resources Institute. IPGRI, Rome, Italy.

Iwanaga, M. 1993. Enhancing links between germplasm conservation and use in a changing world. *In* International crop science I (chapter 52). Crop Science Society of America Inc., Madison, WI, USA.

Joyce, C. 1992. Western medicine men return to the field. BioScience, 42(5), 399.

Juma, C. 1989. Biological diversity and innovation: conserving and utilizing genetic resources in Kenya. African Centre for Technology Studies, Nairobi, Kenya.

Keystone Center. 1991. Final plenary report of the Keystone International Dialogue on Plant Genetic Resources. Kestone Center, Oslo, Norway.

Kloppenburg, J.R., Jr. 1988. First the seed — the political economy of plant biotechnology: 1492–2000. Cambridge University Press, New York, NY, USA.

Lyman, J.M. 1984. Progress and planning for germplasm conservation of major food crops. International Board for Plant Genetic Rsources, Rome, Italy. Plant Genetic Resources Newsletter No. 60.

Morris, D.; Ahmed, I. 1992. The carbohydrate economy. Institute for Local Self-Reliance, Washington, DC, USA.

Mshigenio, K.E. 1990. Foreword. *In* Proceedings of the International Conference on Traditional Medicinal Plants, Arusha, Tanzania, 18–23 February 1990. Ministry of Health, Dar es Salaam, Tanzania.

Mussey, D. 1992. J&J, Merck ready first Euro-brand. Advertising Age, 26 October 1992, p. 1.

Prance, G.T.; Balee, W.; Boom, B.M.; Carneiro, R.L. 1987. Quantitative ethnobotany and the case for conservation in Amazonia. Conservation Biology, 1(4), 296–310.

Quiambao, C. 1992. Good medicine, bitter pill? United Nations Educational, Scientific and Cultural Organisation, Paris, France. Newsletter of the Regional Network for the Chemistry of Natural Products in Southeast Asia, 16(2).

RAFI (Rural Advancement Foundation International). 1993. Bio-piracy: the story of natural coloured cottons in the Americas. RAFI, Ottawa, ON, Canada. RAFI Communique, 1993 (November).

_____1994a. The patenting of human genetic material. RAFI, Ottawa, ON, Canada. RAFI Communique, 1994 (January–February).

_____1994b. "Species" patent on transgenic soybeans granted to transnational chemical giant — W.R. Grace. RAFI, Ottawa, ON, Canada. RAFI Communique, 1994 (March–April).

Reid, W.V. 1993. Biodiversity prospecting: using genetic resources for sustainable development. World Resources Institute, Washington, DC, USA.

Shelton, D. 1993. Legal approaches to obtaining compensation for the access to and use of traditional knowledge of indigenous Peoples. Santa Clara School of Law, University of California, Berkely, CA, USA.

Smith, N.J.H. 1985. Botanic gardens and germplasm conservation. University of Hawaii Press, Honolulu, HI, USA.

Swaminathan, M.S.; Hoon, V. 1994. Methodologies for recognizing the role of informal innovation in the conservation and utilization of PGR: an interdisciplinary dialogue. CRSARD, Madras, India. Proceedings No. 9.

UNEP (United Nations Environment Programme). 1992. Saving our planet: challenges and hopes. UNEP, Nairobi, Kenya.

Unesco (United Nations Educational, Scientific and Cultural Organisation). 1985. UNESCO/WIPO model provisions for national laws for the protection of expressions of folklore against illicit exploitation and other prejudicial actions. Unesco, Paris, France.

UPOV (Union for the Protection of New Varieties of Plants). 1991a. International Convention for the Protection of New Varieties of Plants. UPOV, Geneva, Switzerland.

_____ 1991b. Overview of plant variety protection in the world. In Seminar on the Nature of and Rationale for the Protection of Plant Varieties, Tsukuba, Japan, 12–15 November 1991. UPOV, Geneva, Switzerland.

van Wijk, J.; Junne, G. 1992. Intellectual property protection of advanced technology — changes in the global technology system: implications and options for developing countries. Department of International Relations and Public International Law, University of Amsterdam, Amsterdam, Netherlands.

Waldholz, M.; Stout, H. 1992. Rights to life: a new debate rages over the patenting of gene discoveries (U.S. claim to broad chunks of the human "genome" draws fire from some — the very basis of biotech). The Wall Street Journal, 17 April 1992, p. 1.

Wrage, K. 1994. Patent issued on Pioneer's low-saturated fat high oleic sunflower. Biotech Reporter, 1994 (February), 4.

WRI (World Resources Institute). 1992. Global biodiversity strategy: guidelines for action to save, study, and use the Earth's biotic wealth sustainably and equitably. WRI, Washington, DC, USA.

Yates, M. 1989. Nigerian farmers ply indigenous research approaches. Iowa State University, Des Moines, OH, USA. CIKARD News, 1(2).

About the Institution

The International Development Research Centre (IDRC) is a public corporation created by the Parliament of Canada in 1970 to support technical and policy research to help meet the needs of developing countries. The Centre is active in the fields of environment and natural resources, social sciences, health sciences, and information sciences and systems. Regional offices are located in Africa, Asia, Latin America, and the Middle East.

About the Publisher

IDRC Books publishes research results and scholarly studies on global and regional issues related to sustainable and equitable development. As a specialist in development literature, IDRC Books contributes to the body of knowledge on these issues to further the cause of global understanding and equity. IDRC publications are sold through its head office in Ottawa, Canada, as well as by IDRC's agents and distributors around the world.